BOOK COVER - Credits: NASA, ESA, CSA, STScI; Joseph DePasquale (STScI), Anton M. Koekemoer (STScI), Alyssa Pagan (STScI).

If You Only Knew

Cyde Effect

Copyright © 2023 by Zaid Hameed

All rights reserved. This book or any portion thereof may not be reproduced or used in any manner whatsoever without the expressed written permission of the publisher except for the use of brief quotations in a book review. For permission requests, write to the publisher addressed "Attn: Permissions Coordinator," at the email address below:
EffectivePoetry@gmail.com

Printed in the United States of America First Printing, 2023
ISBN: 9798375529349

"Our Community, Our Responsibility"

From Patterns to Purpose 9

BlackXaid... with an X 12

Weak People 16

Underground Revolution 20

D.T.R. 23

The devil's Advocate 26

Dynasty 29

Black Hystori Project 33

Killmonger / K2(killmonger 2) 38

M'Baku 41

Shuri 43

From Purpose to Service 46

Interview 49

117 54

117 (commentary) 58

Unity 61

Unity (commentary) 64

Peace 68

Peace (commentary) 71

One 74

One (commentary) 77

Success 80

Success (commentary) 83

Intentions 86

Intentions (commentary) 89

Creation 92

Creation (commentary) 96

Faith 101

Faith (commentary) 105

217 107

Warner Brother 110

Warner Brother (commentary) 119

From Patterns to Purpose

Patterns. Patterns of movement, sound, perception, and knowledge are what I've identified as important keys to the foundation of my artistry and growth into higher understanding. Growing up, percussion and beat patterns were of a high interest to me though I'd never formally played any instruments. Besides having grown up listening to all kinds of music including: Hip-hop, Reggae, Jazz, R&B, and Soul; my earliest introduction to the creation of informal patterns could be seen with my activities in guitar club during the sixth grade. Further implementation of patterned performance began as I specialized in the triple jump throughout my time at East Saint Louis Senior High School. During senior year, my interest in structured pattern performance became even more concentrated when I became the Step Master of G5, our school's first step team. The oddity of the step patterns mirrored that of the triple jump as well as off key music performance. Of course I was unaware of these similarities at that time.

It wasn't until I took my first African-American music class at the University of Illinois at Urbana-Champaign that I learned that the term that I sought to identify these patterns was syncopation. I was then able to immediately tie this term into what I love most about all of my favorite music and musical artists. This term is what allows sounds of the same nature yet different structure to fit each other like puzzle pieces. My dad shared that his drum instructor (coincidence) identified this as "adding color" within his instruction. Beforehand, I'd often identified this specialty within one of my favorite hip-hop artists, Common's, music as "rapping southpaw." I identify Kendrick Lamar as also being a heavy influence for my alliteration and multi-syllable rhyme patterns using syncopation or what we called "syllables smashing." One of my other favorite artists at the time as well, Cyhi The Prynce, also heavily utilized syncopation patterns but to a higher degree where he maintained this syncopation structure within the logic of his content, bars, although the content wasn't the purest. All of these examples and then some have combined into the rules of syncopation applied within my poetry to this day. I initially set my goal toward writing so well that any beat would be unnecessary. Essentially, the words themself would be the beat of my poetry. But that goal would only cover the material movement and sound structure of my writing. The perception and knowledge conveyed within my poetry is indeed its higher reality. So the following stories and poems convey my growth into the pure syncopation patterns of that higher reality from their base of material and sound structure. This is how I found purpose in the patterns.

It's October 10th 2015, the date of the 20th anniversary of the Million Man March in Washington DC. The day when I first experienced approximately 1 million black folk in one place at one time; and never felt safer in my life. Thousands of FOIs in their best dress surrounded the crowd "on post" giving the greetings to the many lost founds finding their place amongst each other. Unbeknownst to me, this experience would be one of the key foundations that launched my life in the direction of purpose filled artistry. Artistry rooted in the sacred confines of community meant to instill pride and uplift marginalized minds that share common ground. At this moment in time is when I "thought" I found purpose.

One month later, W.O.R.D (Writers Organizing Realistic Dialect) hosted their semesterly concert for free at the Ike (Ikenberry Commons at the University of Illinois at Urbana-Champaign). I could briefly recall during one of the black freshman introduction programs, Wake Up Call, when W.O.R.D presented and one of the OGs dropped a super fire bar using a hunger games reference. I just didn't know at the time it would take 4 years for me to come back to a W.O.R.D performance. Anyway, I attended not in the interests of poetry, but to support my roommate and homie Chris as he shared some of his writings developed during that semester. Performance after performance passed the stage in front of a packed audience relaying stories in spoken word that kept the crowd active and engaged. Chris's performance had some of the loudest reactions of the entire event. Now I wasn't a hater, but I was definitely competitive enough to state to myself jealously… "I could do that."

Later that month I was made aware that Chris would be performing at an upcoming open mic titled Poetic Justice hosted by UMMA (United Muslim Minority Advocates) before the semester concluded. Being Muslim and relatively involved in campus Muslim activities, I dived headlong into the opportunity to perform the same night as Chris at my first ever open mic. Having been known for my top tier (aka trash) freestyle experience, I concluded that I "think too fast" to write my own poems and needed someone to write them down as I said them. So my good friend and Muslim brother Hussein graciously took on this most honored opportunity because not only is he the top tier writer in our friend circle; but he is also an avid supporter of his good friend's unrealistic goal to be a spoken word poet.

    The poem I wrote casted a wide net that encompassed multiple themes of social justice, personal experience, and unnecessary filler metaphor. But I didn't care, I just wanted to write a poem that could capture my experience of purpose at the Million Man March all while letting everyone know that the Muslim poetry stage should belong to me. So after being introduced to the stage as "Black Zaid" because that's the name assigned to me by the various Middle Eastern and South Asian students of the MSA (Muslim Student Association); I gave a brief correction of my name, for the 100th time, then proceeded to perform the now renamed: BlackXaid…with an X.

BlackXaid... with an X

Deep down I want to change the world
But I want to avoid judgment
Some people may say I'm some things
But deep down I know I wasnt
Until I looked in the mirror and realized that I cant see deep down.
Only the surface, thats all they can see
And realized my skin color is my only purpose
An advancement in society, a new Africa of some sorts
Thats what I want
But thats something that cant be attained
By just going to the Kendrick Concert

I want to make a difference
Not at, but in ground zero
My intentions have never once been to be the hero.
Sometimes a hero is defined by just his actions
And not his intentions
Some people think the he just wants a few mentions
When in fact he knows his people deserve a better position
How do you know that his goal is for others and not himself
When he drops his original career plans
And replaces them with his people
He has just made them more valuable
Than any connotation of wealth

Cause I am from where they're from
The streets
But never dropped beats
I'm like Lebron James
Even 2 years without a ring
I'm still the champ and never flopped heat

On 10 10 2015 I embarked on a journey to Washington DC
This trip was for others and not just for me
It was for a people back home that aren't able to see
That even though we don't have chains anymore, we still ain't free

I came to conclusions in the back of my mind
That in order to produce freedom for my kind
I have to make change in the ways that I go day to day
And some may be confused in what I'm about to say
But we don't have enough leaders to carry us through

Open your eyes I'm telling the truth
I've made the decision emancipate my mind
Lincoln wasn't on our side, so get out of those times
King died for nothing Malcolm died for nothing
Black people walking around with their nose up stuntin
They call me Zaid, no false names, no frontin
Mental slavery is real
But it should've never existed

But Fox news and CNN just so happened to have missed it
There's a war going on and not just amongst the people
There's a higher power tellin us that we're not the ones that's evil
But yall killed off so many of my people
That the Black man is going extinct like the bald eagle
We need more leaders and a lot less cheaters
Too many men are stuck following b******
When that term for our women should have never even existed
We need to start following our women
Because according to Minister Farrakhan
They are second to G-d
So instead of running game you need to the run to the mosque
Because I'm already there leading the charge

I am from East St Louis Illinois
Ironically where I'm from,
Many didn't have air conditioning
But everyone had heaters
Yes, that is a real place
It's dangerous in those streets,
And I walked them day to day
Not knowing at any moment my life could be taken away
But I had a foundation that wasn't available for a lot of people in my situation
Every single day I dreamt of taking a vacation

Back in 99 I remember always playing playstation
Not knowing my parents were keeping me safe in the basement
From the guns blazing outside
From my people that were given stressful placement
Playin basic shooters in the game
Not realizing that the player I was controlling was outside
With his life on the line against his own kind
But because I chose to rhyme, I made up my mind
That I want to do better things

But like an angel without its wing
Will I only fall?
Or will I spread a word so powerful
That it inspires the people behind me to excel beyond these walls
Because there is no such thing as a border
That can suppress an oppressed people in distress feeling depressed….
I digress

In hindsight, a review of my first-ever poem would not be the greatest. But from where I stand today, I can only see it as a seed of potential. What that potential is capable of growing into is clearly evident in my current writings. What followed my performance for some reason was feedback on how I responded to the "black Zaid" introduction on stage. Those conversations and others persuaded me to begin writing my next poem to be titled "Weak People"; in recognition of my then favorite artist Cyhi The Prynce's similarly named song. I consider "Weak People" to be my true first poem because I actually wrote it without any assistance in January 2016.

Weak People

I have made it to my last threads
You peoples minds is past dead
The weakness is too abundant
And hides as passive
Just ask Rev,
I hope you got a spiritual leader,
You got your girl to follow you but aint got the Spirit to lead her
Because you a mental cheater
Not knowing your selfishness only defeats her
You try to barely pep her only to slice up her mind like some pizza,

Grow a backbone or try to get a spine
Open up your eyes and realize everything aint fine
Don't be a slave try to be brave
Be an example to show the future generations have to behave
Don't be a b**** and always stand up quick
Think it's all good, I'll slow it down is case your skull is too thick

I aint the s***
I've just been thinkin
look at the clueless sitting around you
Dumbfounded with their eyes bulged blinkin
I'm sick and tired of people saying I speak out too much
For me to believe
You've never seen anything ignorant would be dumb as ****
So I don't believe it
You just choose not to see it
Little do you know one day you're going to be it
"But you'll say oh no I'm a good person"
Oh yeah you didn't do the shooting,
But youre the actor playing the part of
Driving the body to the grave again
Dress rehearsing

Peoples pupils mute the realistic mutual
Thoughts and visuals the make living useful
Meaning you're too busy slaving and behaving
As though your purpose is not for chasing
A mystic Ideology like the masons
You're too busy flinching and bracing
When you could be in leading the charge
Transporting the people like Jason Statham

To all the brown nosers and their fellow kiss a*****
When your massas aint here
Who's really gonna lead your classes....
Because masters don't lead
They just succeed with greed
And then here comes you sheep
Eating his s*** disguised as feed
Hard work and dedication
Don't forget the motivation
Build the bridge for better placement
Then bring your people for preservation
So if you fall you'll receive resuscitation
Until the day you all reach the haven

So when is silence is consent a true a*** statement
When you realize that you're mentally locked in the basement
Your greedy hopes and dreams are just the rats you're chasing
Brand new clothes and shoes are just things that spiders are lacing
And that dirty glass mirror you cant even see your face in
But we all even you have great potential
That mirror does not represent the cleanliness of your soul
It represents the cloudiness of your mind and how easy it is to fold
So wipe off that damn mirror And take a deep look inside
Realize the reason you're in the basement is just too hide
There is no shame in having just a little pride

But don't let it get to your head otherwise youll remain the problem
One of the weak people, with mental locks and we wont solve em
Too busy trying to be part of the popular solution by dissolving

But don't you know youre supposed to be the solution and not the solvent
The difference between the two spans
From being just a watcher to having true involvement

My team cant consist of weak people
For they serve no purpose to my mission
They be dismissing and omitting clear visions
While assisting the mental lynchings of a people missing
Thats something I'm not feeling
For the facts of some of them not just justifying
But admiring the killing
It don't even have to be that deep in order to absorb that fully,
I had to correct someone nicely
For introducing me as black Zaid on stage
And for some reason I still got called a bully

But you know what
If you don't expect anything then you wont be disappointed
So weak people,
I stopped expecting s*** from you a long time ago
SO SURPRISE ME

By the time Weak People was written and completed, I'd joined W.O.R.D and began working with Chris and using his experience to help strengthen my writings. I was able to perform Weak People in front of 100+ students, faculty, and staff during that February's Black and Latino Male Summit. As the Spring 2016 semester proceeded, I became more and more confident in my performance and creative expression. I was then able to write and memorize two additional pieces with my groups for the upcoming semester concert titled "Underground." I was proudly able to perform a group piece titled "Underground Revolution" and another titled "UnderGround Kings" with Chris and a couple other W.O.R.D members.

Underground Revolution

As the dark flows ruffle and roll off the tongue
In flocks like a murder of crows, muttering flows,
No shoes, mud on the toes,
The black man took flight... Officer Jim murdered the crow

While ceasing potential, reaping stencils
Teasing and ceasing construction
Making a searing blaring crevice
Increasingly creeping as clinical corruption
Why must I give a damn about the feelings of the weak people
Harriet said she would shoot them
When they wanted to go back South
And just like then today slavery is still legal
While we're pushing impassively lasting
Radical staggering verbs down the avenue
Forcing knowledge down the throat
And cracking already broken souls without fracturing clavicles

The feeling that I expressed in Weak People was anger,
Because you treat your fellow brothers
And especially sisters not as an equals
But as a strangers
We are Kings and Queens
But don't romanticize the visions
For just as the n*****
The Negus
Continually populate the prisons
Cause thats the systems vision

Even in this realm
Everyone needs a mother to love and nourish them,
Just as from Underground
The largest tree nourishes its smallest stem,

Use your platform to speak the truth like Steven Salaita
For who gave you all the privilege
To be just writers and not a freedom fighters
You're too busy writing with no purpose to the masses
When you need to express your words to the current masters
So we can get our masters
And steal the higher classes

So no longer the powers at be
Can turn us around and kick the black peoples a****
To sustain ourselves we need the main course and not just the rations
Cause some pastor's passion
Is bashing the black man for gain with no action
These factions then factor in false rap sins with fatal retractions
These are the facts that kill us as we trap with straps called Mack 10's
No sins just wins from the beginning to the end

But even the lost ones have a purpose
Even if thats just to purchase
Maan even hearses are almost always
Guaranteed to contain a person
So are you gonna continue to allow situations to worsen
Or will you embrace new nurturing black nationalist
Methods to prevent negative negro coercion

Because this story is detailing the consistent themes within my growth into pure syncopation patterns portraying growth in perception and knowledge, trust me, UnderGround Kings was not progressive nor the type of content I would want to circulate within environments of spiritual development. Which is a significant point to take note of, when combined with the fact that our group won Favorite Piece, and I won the Show Up & Show Out award for that performance during the semesterly awards. In hindsight, I've learned that regressive themes in art and poetry have just as much potential for receiving recognition as progressessive themes. Luckily I was growing out of those forms of expression as well as beginning to use less profanity.

All thanks and praise due to The Most High, I took that energy and experience gained from the spring concert and aimed it toward the fall W.O.R.D concert with the intention of igniting an expression directed at Donald Trump and white supremacy furthering my growth and not settling for regressive themes. While spending time with the homie Hussain, I came up with the phrase "My very presence in this room is resistance." This theme was to encompass the idea of how a black student simply sitting in a majority white or any classroom exudes a form of resistance without need of any other action. I told Hussein that I would create an entire poem with this theme and perform it as a solo for the fall W.O.R.D concert. Fast forward, I was able to open the entire concert, themed "The Purge", with this poem D.T.R (Definition of Tempting Resistance) while also performing a group piece later that evening titled "The devil's Advocate" written from the perspective of a black police officer that didn't know that he was black.

D.T.R

My very presence in this room as resistance
I raise hell to your heaven
To the point where your privilege
Makes you feel devilish in this existence
Don't question my persistence
The definition of resistance is the radical form of defensive
As well as being the offensive form facing false fences
Unfulfilled fasting faces feel faithfully fake and wasted
Mistakenly taking breaks
When Brock Turner is gettin away with r****g
He's a manifestation of what the white man gets away with
Around the world and not just in this nation

Exhaling Society sickening scientific syphilis
Through cigarettes disguised as vaping
Revolution with that retribution
Makes it evident that we pursue lasting movements
Ceasing confusion with an ideological illusion
Every once in a blue moon a new coon
Will soon promise an impossible conclusion
And too late
We'll learn that pimping your people
Is now a form of cultural prostitution

But you can't pimp me
I'm not a butterfly
I'm not a new coon
I'm just a cocoon avoiding fumes of the establishment
I wasn't from that side of the streets
So I never had to bust a cap in it
But I was broke so I could never put stacks on it
Mugs will only criticize when
They don't think youre passionate
But yall mugs gone be mad
When I sit my a** down like Kaepernick

Exist to resist that list that they fixed
To prevent our race shift toward the bliss
I aint deep
But why do they call it Wake Up Call when
Folks walk out of Foellinger still sleep
I aint miss the call at all
But yall act small
When 10,000 fearless can make a resolve

My melanin makes me wish I got sunshine on a cloudy day
My girl dares for solidarity everyday
Why do people need an explanation?
This aint just my imagination
Let me give you the definition of temptation

Temptation is another white student
Assuming I'm just another black factor
Temptation is another white student
Thinking I'm a slave and their my master
I would say that mug need a pastor
But they'll just use the Bible justification
That the blacker tone has the cursed blood of HAM in the bone
Racist tendencies commanded 10 times engraved in stone
These are the manipulated messages from the white man's dome

Start the metronome
The ignorance of dome has dimly shown
That the futures flock has flown
Downward with the quickness of chrome
The quickness of a bullet from chrome to dome
Causes the phone to roam as you attempt to phone home
Though I am their leader
I'm not reliant on the ignorance that fuels the weak people
No discretion
Their perceptions contain deception
Sleeping through this system shows their mind is incepted
Selfishly protecting they pensions
They mental pistils be pumping like pistons
Did I mention

The chains have been transformed into links for the fences
Silence is still consent when you're blind to evident tensions
Yeah I'm talking bout Clinton,
The super predator princess
I call her Cersi cause she's Joffrey Trumps evil apprentice

My people locked up behind bars but still renting
Not even supposed to be missing
The cops be steppin on your fresh kicks whenever they friskin

So now we in the streets dodging bullets like the matrix
The police trying to test me
But they don't know I got some patience
I don't want to be another body
In the hospital around the doctors and patients
Barely got any money to keep my lights on
But for this bail I still gotta pay cents
I'd much rather not be downtown with the pigs in they station
Got me hoping for a prayer
But for now I know that I'm faithless

I am a poet whose purposeful poetic poems
Place a peaceful push to painfully purge
Through the vicious verbs while still unheard
But where is the one place I know that I'm heard
The one place I know can contain a true verse
The place where there's no resistance
If I were to express through a curse
It has always been said to keep your family first
I swear I'm more loyal to W.O.R.D
Than I am to the church

But this has just been my verse through a striving resisting serge
This has been the Definition of Tempting Resistance
But for you its the start of the Purge
But It turns out I never uttered a word
So for now, I'm still unheard

The devil's Advocate

Sir
Do you know why I pulled you over today
Move slowly not boldly
Kkeep your hands where you can show me
Do I smell pot
Just like in the street
Hands on the wheel
Before I make you Holy
Now reach for your ID
Why you shakin
I thought you were of righteous men
But evidently just like Ali you have parked-in-sin
Hold up
Look at me
Sir
Do you know why I pulled you over today
I'm an enforcer of a system
That treats you as a stain on my apron
That I purge like prey

If I smell weed
You bleed
Because implicit bias disguised as racism is indeed my creed
I'm assuming you're another creepin criminal
Cruising and confusing us good cops
You dont even know my actions are subliminal
Serving death to you like the seminoles
As I choke you and you screech I can't breathe
I know,
I just have to remind you your kind ain't freed

Why are you being pulled over?
You dont need to know that
Give me your license
I may take something away from your life that's priceless

I'll make you wish that you
Believed in something more righteous
God Bless America
But when in my custody you are now rights-less
Because your dark skins a sin that blends in the wind
To deepen the need for amends, **** that
Let me grab my gun and step back

I think I'm doing the right thing
Cops have been around for centuries right
Patrolling the world keeping the street safe day and night
From the criminals scheming
Because they don't have the privilege of the white
Paving pathways to push plentiful
Possibilities of the future toward the light
But yalls very presence in my presence is resistance
I see you as weak people
But for some reason you see me as weaker
I was causing blood to drip
In your own street as though I was a beaker

From my perspective you're kind is defective
Cause you lack corrective pretentious perceptions
Transform the mentality its a mendable reality
Except its exponentially expendable
Not dependable
I'll bloody you son
Thats the end
PERIOD
White men still rule

Have you been drinking this evening??
Of course you were driving straight
But answer me wrong and I'll send your a** to heavens gate
My wife and kids expect me to return home safe
No one knows I beat them like I beat you
Maybe I'll lock you up
With a combination of house arrest plus death in your own place
So you can return home safe

Here I was, one year later writing and performing my own pieces on the same stage that inspired me to begin writing in the first place. Though I was new to the performance scene, because of my writing experience, confidence, and super senior status, amongst my new campus artist community I was already considered a W.O.R.D OG. During the semester awards I won the "Palm Tree Award" for being the most petty because let's be honest, roasting was in my DNA. The following January, Team Backpack hosted a series of events back home in the St. Louis area where they partnered with my fellow artist and Muslim brother Mvstermind which included an underground performance / Cypher type of event. Toward the end of this event I took the opportunity to perform DTR for the crowd. Little did I know that this would be my first performance in the Saint Louis music scene which will be more detailed in just a bit.

Back on campus it was my last semester, W.O.R.D began to experience its own revolution conducted between its members and its board. The bullying of members by the board, combined with favoritism, and performance censorship led to this type of division. It manifested in one of the female members performing an unapproved piece directed toward one of the board members in traditional battle rap fashion during a group piece that concluded the entire show. Chris and I were a part of this group piece trio where I concluded the entire show with my piece. Chris and I both knew that this pivot may occur and gave our permission for it to be used in the final performance of our collegiate poetry careers. Because we knew it was justified and we refused to stand in the way of an artist's expression. The theme of the show was Pandora's Box and the name of this group piece was Dynasty. Dynasty was themed after a collegiate probate but instead of unveiling ourselves as Greeks, we unveiled ourselves as Poets. I also had the opportunity to perform in another group piece titled Black Hystori Project. Black Hystori Project was written to express how the word Hotep and individuals considered "hoteps" needed to be separated in order to maintain the relevancy and positive attributes of the word. This was achieved by expanding upon other areas of black history outside of Egypt that may not be as commonly known.

Dynasty

Welcome to the probate
No literally
If y'all didn't know it
This is bait for pros
Im talking professional poets

I am Z
Surrounded by fighters
Against freezing forces
Fighting remorseless
In numbers enormous
No talking
I'm not playing
I am Goku in formation at the Super Bowl man
Im beyond Saiyan

I learned from Kendrick back in the purple lean van
Sherane killed my vibe in the back seat
Using a freestyle of peer pressure
Money Trees couldn't provide
A Poetic type of Justice for a Good kid in a Maad City
Avoiding deadly stressors
In the swimming pool still dying of thirst
Recognizing real n***** from Compton to bompton
Are still diasporic treasures

Cornrow Kenny got me crip walking on payday
Don't you know how they coerced the n******
Back in the slave day
They'd give em a milli to rock with the fact
That they whipped his girl Nae Nae

A poet's-purpose
Is to, know what's worthless
Not to, judge the verses
That the, purses-purchase
Just to, serve the servants
Serving purple curses
To just nurture nurses
Moving persons hearses
To write perfect verses
For pre-serving persons
-
A poetic surgeon will serve up versions
Avoiding murky murder
So he can perm the perverts
Tighten down the lines
Yo peep the girder
Thats me

theBARista
Here to release the
Bars of the trap to free the bees and please them
Not cease them
Allow them to achieve their degrees and freedom
Student of kendrick
Never finished

Sinners salty like ramen
I don't even know why half of them started rhyming
I learned from the rap gods Kendrick, Cyhi, Common
That if you want to relate to the weak people
First you gotta find something in common
So you can cause their minds to shine bright like a diamond
No rihanna

So can a bar get me a bae tho
Let me tell you about my personal life
The difference is black and white like a panda
I was so broke that I studied abroad in Atlanta
That girl was a trip

So did a bar get me a bae tho?
No
But I'm still philosophically non-toxic like Plato
Yall protesting a brothers perception of a perfect direction
Flaunting a failing false reflection

Here we go again with that syllable ish
Walking around like he lyrical and ish
Yo check the checklist
My flows are reckless
I guess that's why I'm checkless,
But check this out
Since got want a death wish
I'll put you in check
And check you in
Leaving you living while you dead and breathless

These were Cynical Statements
Based in a place that is pinnacle placement
Where we're pacing and racing the ruthless races
Ruining our stasis
This is 2 stories I'm trapped in a box that has a basement
Some have to pop acid to get to where I'm based in
But my bars so hard you'd need the strength of Mike Colter
If you Luke at what I was caged in

But I came back to free my people
So how fast am I moving when I break in?
As fast as forest gump without the Jenny
Competition?
Other poets?
If I see any Ima kill em like I killed Kenny
Young muslim boy don't need no henny
I'm more designer than prada gucci and fendi

When writing lines my neutrons and Johns be driving faster than Jimmy's
And if you're wondering
Just ask Stevie
John Cena cant see me

I'm gonna be better than both Wayne and Drake
Believe me
Bars so arrogant its funny how they lack humility
I'm steaming up this room raising the heat and humidity
Yall call this a party in a large vicinity
I represent an entire continent
Comprised of melanin and turnt up cultural amenities
Times infinity
Man stop offending me
G-d already sent his last prophet
But wound up still sending me

Black Hystori Project

You ever wake up in the middle of the night hot
Cuz it's 97 degrees
And you smell the funk of the master
Flexing his strength over slaves
While their bowing on their knees

Just tryna clear your mind
Waiting on summer time cuz you hear the blood on the leaves
Engulfed in fire
Standing not at ease
Drawing flames like Liu Kang with a pen filled with either
The fire of the diaspora is telling you to e a strong leader
Not a people pleaser
Pathetically leasing your cultures mental features
As though they're creatures
So what can you teach us

You sound like you want to be hurting me
Emmanual asked then Aza stated
There ain't no more leaders
Just uncle Toms and deceivers
Focused on their personal gain and careers
Afraid to face their fears
These n***** ain't got no gas
They roll through the revolution in a Prius

So what you're saying is
Greatness doesn't only lie In the minds
Of those that think they're consciousness is clearer
Africa is vast
And Kemet represents way more than what's just
Northeast of the Sahara
Some want to challenge and manipulate
Us and our ancestors mission
Omitting the many tribal lines still existing

No longer contorting cultural ties
You see in the FOI
My folks was bow twisting

The new school of thought
Wait
We on the grind during lunch time
Food for thought
Making your mind-full with bean pies for consumption

These new coons and they conclusions
They see us
Baptist Protestants and Lutherans
Sunnis Shiites and Sufis
As Religious cultural rufis
And then want us to be clueless
And act like Jesus wasn't Jewish
Preaching the Gospel

Descendant from Ethiopia
Africa's uncolonized utopia
2000 years later we got the Rastas
Following the word of Garvey to Haile Selassie
Preaching peace as they smoke the herb to the ashes
Releasing their mind from the confines of the Masters
Cleansing critical creative cultural clans
Masa Musa on the pilgrimage traversed miles across the sands
Sayyida the pirate queen of North Africa
Ruled the Moroccan city Tetouan
So don't act as though a woman couldn't beat the best man

The culture if flipped it is turning
Facing fellowship lift then its burning
No one is learning
Warning Warning
We up in the fields farming,
In formation facing the past that is haunting the strong in us
Fear in ourselves don't belong in us
The sands of time to us is more than dust
Prince of Persia

Nonchalant Prince of Conscious
Causing catastrophic Nauseous nonsense,
Cynical Savior of the south side
Like I got Communal Consensus with comm sense

So when it comes to our culture
Don't put her at the back of ya mind like Rosa
Ruby bridges walked into the education system with a soldier
And thats the truth
Educate the youth
We not just kings and queens
We are miracles by G-d given more power than zeus

I'm an original not operating through the shadows
Meaning no matter how privileged I become
I wont forget about the fight back in the ghettos
Showing that black panther aint one of the only black superheroes
Straight up human metamorphosis
Im a contortionist
I am Neo
I am One
With the wisdom of morpheus
Black thought in the mind causing mental nuclear fusion
Sojourner Truth with Tariq and the roots is my religion
Avoiding governmental systematic distortions

Woke goals
This is food for the soul
Take control of your portions
Hold the hypocrites highly for their heinous habitual extortion
Reigning rigor on resources
Defining intercultural forces
Denying the influx of Afro courses
Silencing sentimental urban sources

Then that causes the progress to cease
So I end with Salaam
Or Peace
Hotep
To be at peace with yourself

Don't let that word lose its meaning
Yes, the culture is diasporic
So remember its the ignorant folks not the word that needs cleaning
So don't be demeaning if you don't know the meaning

After graduation I began working back home in the St. Louis area. Over the next year-and-a-half I began getting my feet wet in the underground artist community. Most significantly as the merchandise manager of Mvstermind and as founder and CEO of my own mobile app development company YoDJ. YoDJ allows DJs to accept song requests at any performance venue while also accepting tips to play those requests. Along with meeting DJs as a part of Mvstermind's team, I also took the initiative of meeting Open Mic DJs by also breaking the ice with my poetry by performing those nights. Though I was only recirculating my collegiate poetry, I was still able to make significant connections that lead toward growth of both YoDJ and my public poetry presence. During this time I was known as The BARista and HAMZ as I had never focused on a stage name, but HAMZ eventually stuck. HAMZ was a nickname I kept since high school that was a combination of my last name and first initial. I was also known as DJ HAMZ during my time as an on-air radio and podcast host in college.

As I became more well-known across the St. Louis poetry scene, I came to the conclusion that my collegiate and early STL poetry lacked cohesiveness, story progression, and focused topics. What I've identified as the higher realities of syncopation. With that understanding, I felt that by attaching my stories to narratives already known that I could help my writing increase toward these goals. This process began with my poem Killmonger in January 2019. It was quickly followed by the completion of M'baku and Shuri. This trilogy of poetry encompassing the theme and energy of the Black Panther movie expressed an exponential growth in the cohesive impactfulness of my poetic storytelling. Though my name was still HAMZ, I began to be known as Killmonger across the St. Louis poetry scene.

Killmonger / K2(killmonger 2)

I am an African descendant storyteller
When things fall apart
I'm like Okonkwo in Wakanda
Caught hot handed with a pot grinder
Got reprimanded with a purple herb
That the king handed to me
In a tea heated and steaming like a hot sauna

Is this your king?
Cause I'm not T'Challa,
I'm N'Jadaka the Killmonger
A skilled hunter expressing real hunger
Make the prey pray and wait in fear just to live longer
Willing to kill and Klaue my way to the point
I could enter the real Wakanda

A place where greatness is honored
From Addonis to Donda
Where we don this fit that are not designer nor laundered
There off a long list
Back when santa delivered sandals and saunas
To wakanda vacay destinations upon us, I ponder?

In a cultural wonderland where we can keep our culture honest
Where no one knows who glows the brightest till they start to blind us
Where we promote dope votes to see whos coconut fros grow the finest
And at the end of the day
No one's allowed to console the diamonds,
Cause we already sold the diamonds
To the negative black folks that already stole the diamonds
Stuck on the last line then here's your soul assignment
Complete this test then after death youll know your souls assignment
Negative black equals white

Thats the whole assignment
That last line wasn't an attack or supposed to be violent
Just a natural abstract based in a coal hard facts
Thats the soul of diamonds

Thats why I was formed by pressure
Thats the message
This piece is a brief session of my mind
Expressing already evident scripture
So I guess I'm guess I'm kinda like Wakanda
A motion picture
Disguised as a cultured hipster
Exposing fitna
Exposing the cracks like a frozen fissure

Matter fact now I got work in the morning
Projecting the image that I am over performing
Knowing I'm no better that a quote on quote
Bum in the slums or on the corner snoring
But to you that's a warning
To watch out for poets
Hey Auntie, Killmonger is a new form of Prince Charming
I just hope you know it

-(K2)-

But I hope no one knows about this gat that
He tote for potus (he = killmonger the character)
Ittl paint the rose garden red without the roses
With a noose composed of hoses...
He'll hang around & spray down the line of succession
Like he washing clothing

I'm openly tryna promote the notion
That every other pig's blood is a toxic potion
That's why cops cock-block locked and loaded
They ******* the streets over and not rocking trojans

In this piece I've already stopped breathing
Expressing the feelings of my

Great-great-great-granddaddy a slave named Moses Beaman
I bet he had more anger than this
When he was seeking his freedom
Trying to deceive and then leave the demons
Back when following the prophet had a different meaning

Check the moves that I'm making
YoDJ thats my bread baby
A funding source that I'm baking
Funds for the non-privileged patrons facing the nation
So Zaid can finally go off and take a vacation
See I started to create with creators
To follow waves to one day make it a mission
Connect all the bosses
Make the Midwest competition
Against the east and west coast I'm talking a coalition
Oh I ain't folding
I'm still bringing hope to the hopeless
Home alone smoking the doping
Like the homie Macaulay Culkin
I'm saiyan
Just like Sonic going golden
But I'm holding a hundred holy tokens
While I'm tellin you Tails about my Knuckles being broken

If the broke dont cope with life's lows
Then the soul goes cold
As they emotions blow when the pipes frozen
Tell me what notes on your mind are you not composing

M'Baku

Where lies the fate of the man-ape
Bound to rampage and reign outrageous
See aint no mountain high enough
To stop a King with a dream to scheme out of the cages
Then wait on top watching...
Ready to march down with his patrons

After the winter soldier emboldened
A prince to seek revenge when his father was taken
Tradition makes it the way that I can say its challenge day
Cause now the throne is for the taking...
I… The leader of the Jabari... Am on a safari...
To become king so rejoice yet hardly party

To me everyday is a challenge…
And if its to a prince then I'm hardly sorry
I can stand tall and say this surely...
I'll take your throne then this man-ape
Will then-take the hand-of-and marry Shuri
From our mountain tops to your Wakandan plots and places
I scoff at new traditions and take shots in stages
For I feel our ancestors hate to watch the vibranium wasted

And your father was never the King of the mountain pouncing;
Not even climbing…
I heard it was your fault that he was lion and dying like Mufasa
When the scars dropped him
After the blast when signing accords at the Sokovia conference
As the freedom bells ring
tThis is the return of the King prophesied by the Rastas
I am M'Baku
The Jabari Selassie

I'll be a king that fights to prevent the return of the masters
My passion yearns to burn and become the black panther
Thank God I am not you...
Just because youre alive that doesn't mean we forgot you
We'll still free the blood from our enemies like Nosferatu
I say we will not have it as I'll proudly issue a challenge to stop you

Walking strong as stone like a statue to the throne I block you
With my Queen on my side... so just know that we will rock you...
Bringing a breath of fresh air
But I'll beat you till you cant breathe through your nostrils
Unlike you I'll know the proper way to deal with imposters
I woulda made sure that the border tribe killed N'Jadaka
So we would've never had to know the name of Eric Killmonger
And infinity war wished it had a scene in Wakanda

See thats a place where greatness is honored
From the mountain tops to bottoms
Got imposters playin possum cause we stopping problems
Shid... We made the moon dark with an ark
Before the start of the rocket launches
Eatin Wakandan Jollof lunches
With plenty of cash in our pockets

Your own business you mind it
Cause we're past the time of the pocket watches
All of that is what I can promise...
Winston Duke presents...
A Jabari future to the panther pupils
Then M'Baku tapped out...
So this whole piece was useless

Shuri

Wakanda is the model that molded me to be cohesive
From N'Jadaka the Killmonger, M'Baku and the K2 Thesis
I've been writing nonstop with no plans on ceasing
Now, presenting a piece portrayed as Princess Letitia

A miracle making kid genius
In brown skin an African features
Teaching science and technology in crafted speeches
Engineering and mathematics
After practice help to master habits
For the passionate princess living in the panther palace...
So finally
Here's a black girl bringing some blacker magic
Cause all that old Harry Potter ish is caste backwards...
No more nerdy white boys in bad fashion
Feeling asthmatic in cracked glasses
Now its hidden figures
Figuring ways to use their minds to surpass Nasa
With natural curls locd laced and baby hairs laid a tad backwards

She's the next black woman in charge of saving the vision
The next up in a long lineage of the world's greatest women
I need you to sit and look not just listen
There's an art to locking down bars without guarding a prison...
When her brothers off on a mission
Guess whos running the business
Sharing their tech through the outreaching centers
M'Baku back off... She respect the traditions
Check this fit and wit that our ancestors gifted
T'Challa made you submit so now you're forced to bear witness
A panther sit on a throne surrounded by sisters

Livin life like a type of ambassador
Proof that black girls rock from Oakland to Africa
And just like Toph… She's a metal bending master
With the vibranium blasters
As her brother reps the mantle of king and the Black Panther...
Stan Lee crafted for Ryan Coogler a character
Mastered by the actress...
Letitia Wright a teach you right before you land in a casket…

I wanted to send off this series like a right of passage
Thinking about her made me blush as I write my passage
Is this the ending to the Black Panther trilogy
That I established???
Just wait for the sequel
Her IQ... Above average
Beyond cameras and black fashion
Her art game includes black dances performed with passion
Giving me outstanding reasons to redefine my standards
Then I shot my shot wrong though I own 2 cameras

I guess it's all got to come to an end of some sort
Guess I gotta lawyer up to learn how to court
Always stay respectful and have no fury
Let this case now close with the verdict set by the jury
As I still ask that question
Where will I find my Shuri?

In Wakanda...
A place where greatness is honored
And thats a Promise

My year-and-a-half on the St Louis poetry scene culminated into this trilogy. Summer 2019 I was blessed with the opportunity to perform on the St Louis poetry slam team as well as in another poetry slam as an individual. Killmonger was put to the test on both of these stages. It's safe to say that Killmonger & Shuri did not succeed competitively. But little did I know, they along with their trilogy were the seed for my next stage of development as a poet. This was also the year that I met and got to share the stage with my two favorite poets Brandon Alexander Williams and T Spirit.

On the back end of that summer, a significant life altering event occurred that founded the current phase of my life both as an individual and as an artist. I would go into additional detail of that experience, but every poem and expression that follows in this story, this book, and my life formed from the details of that experience. Its detail lies within all of my current personal and artistic expressions. Shuri would be the last poem that I completed before entering a year-and-a-half long writer's block that ended August 2020 with my poem 117. This period of writer's block consisted of hundreds and hundreds of hours of deep meditation, self reflection, writing, and eventually deep scriptural study. At its end I was able to confidently say that my patterns had finally arrived at the foot of purpose.

From Purpose to Service

أَشْهَدُ

ASH HADU
(I Openly Bear Witness)

لَا إِلَٰهَ إِلَّا ٱللَّهُ

AN LA ILLAHA ILLALLAH
(That There is No G-d Except Allah)

وَأَشْهَد

WA ASH HADU
(And I Openly Bear Witness)

أَنَّ مُحَمَّدًا رَسُولُ ٱللَّهِ

ANA MOHAMMED DAN RASUL ALLAH
(That Mohammed Is The Messenger of Allah)

When the age-old question is asked, if you could go back in time and meet your younger self, what advice would you give? My answer would be, If You Only Knew. If You Only Knew your true purpose when you were on your initial journey, where would you be now? If You Only Knew that by releasing any sense of control you felt you had in your life to the Originator of the Heavens and the Earth would provide you a sense of fulfillment and completion during all stages of your journey, would you do it? If You Only Knew that all of your life experiences were designed in such a way that communicates your nature and destination, would you believe it?

Our purpose lies in service. Service to our Creator first. But how do you serve a Creator that is in need of no service? By serving what that Creator would want you to serve, which is It's Creation. This service is worship, this service is work, this service is preservation, this service is development. This service is protection, provision, and maintenance. Of course at the foot of purpose I did not know all of this, but I definitely knew what it would take to get there and that I was just at the beginning. I'd known that I'd been provided a second chance and did not want to waste the opportunity to perform most excellently.

This book, If You Only Knew, is my service to believers, seekers, and beings yearning to recognize how the story of their life's development is a road map and guide for finding their purpose. Just as my poems have been formed, you can then mold your purpose into a service that can both benefit and sustain yourself and all of creation.

If You Only Knew (21:7)

إِن كُنتُمْ لَا تَعْلَمُونَ

(In KuunTuum La T'alemuun)

      The following poems represent how the principles of Kwanzaa when articulated through their shared Islamic term can each communicate "If You Only Knew" to my younger self and you. Swahili being a trade language of East Africa with the Semitic language of the Arabs, Arabic, simplifies this logic. To communicate G-d consciousness during this age of contradictory influence is a task not to be taken lightly. G-d Consciousness conveyed by way of action is exemplified in the life model and example of many of our most cherished leaders, historical figures, and artists. Muslims specifically, reflect upon and honor the life model and example demonstrated by Mohammed the Prophet (peace be upon him). We are to live our lives according to The Holy Qur'an and its miraculous text. I strive to consciously ensure that all of my poems develop as a complementary expression for the excellence of our human nature to exemplify G-d consciousness. All errors and faults are my own and any good that is expressed or received is due only to Allah.

Scan for full playlist

Interview

Brandon Alexander Williams: We're sitting here with a great Cyde Effect from East St. Louis, Illinois. I'm your host, Brandon Alexander Williams, we're gonna get into this album **If You Only Knew**, but before we do, how are you feeling man?

Cyde Effect: Man, All Praise to The Most High (Alhamdulillah) I am well, it's a nice chilly Friday. Just flew in from the A recently moved down in the last year to be married to my beautiful wife Jayda, who is joining us in the studio today. But we got to fly in today, got in this morning, got to rent a very nice car because I'm not here that long. See some family later, but you know, I'm at peace.

Brandon Alexander Williams: That's what's up man, congratulations. I'm gonna put a sound bite right there of like an audience clapping when you say *get married*, shout out to the married folk, you know what I'm saying? So let me ask you a couple more things before we get into this first track. So when did we meet again? We met here in St. Louis.

Cyde Effect: We met in St. Louis. Brandon Alexander Williams was performing for Poetic Justice open mic at the Grandel. I don't know if you were featuring or not. I just know when you performed on stage, I was like, he writes like me, you know, it's a very unique lane of spoken word poetry, slash, it's rapping, it's rappy, but it's spoken word and I don't see that often. And I was walking around the city with my new Killmonger poem, I think it was like spring 2019 or something like that. And I went up to Brandon while he was selling the red book outside and I was like, yo, I'm gonna do this poem, I want you to listen to it because you know, poets love to be heard.

Brandon Alexander Williams: Word.

Cyde Effect: We just wanna be heard, right? I ain't expecting nothing. Did you hear me though? Cool. Peace.

Brandon Alexander Williams: Yeah, I was refreshed because you were dope. Because like sometimes I'll get cats who like, oh, let you hear peace or whatever and so I was excited. I was gonna listen to you either way, all the way through, but once I made a mental note like, oh no, this is fire. I put it in the back of my brain, like at some point I'm gonna do some type of work with his brother or hire him to speak somewhere. You know what I'm saying? And so no, I want to commend you for your talent man. Let me ask you, where does it come from? Tell me the first piece you wrote? Who are your first influences? Is it rap, is it spoken word? Is it an orator?

Cyde Effect: So at the beginning of the book, I tell a story about going to my first ever spoken word event at the University of Illinois. My roommate Chris was performing, so this is in fall 2015 going in the winter and I ain't know nothing about no poetry, I just went to support the homie. And when I got in there, Chris was dropping bars after bars, after bars on stage. And everybody reacting, crowd reacting and I'm sitting in the crowd like man, I could do that. This is Chris man, come on now. So after that, one month later, one of the Muslim organizations on campus was hosting an open mic called Poetic Justice. Like every open mic is low-key Poetic Justice.

Brandon Alexander Williams: Shoutout to John Singleton.

Cyde Effect: Chris was going to perform there and I was like, I can't have Chris on the Muslim stage, I'm the Muslim around here, this is my opportunity to go show what I could do. So you know, I went there, a homie of mine, Hussein, he helped me write the poem out. Cause I was like, I think too fast, I think too fast to write my poems because you know, I was known for free styling and I wasn't that good. I was not that good. My favorite freestyle Instrumental was *Let Nas Down* by J Cole, that beat to freestyle, I thought yo, this is the best beat of all time. But looking back, whew, that was a different time. Anyway, Hussein wrote the piece out for me while I was saying it, he added like two lines in there and I went and performed it, and got introduced on stage as Black Zaid. That's a whole other thing. I was like, it's just Zaid and did it, people said it was good. I mean, I looked at the video and watched it years later and was like, ah. But one month later I wrote, what I consider my first poem because I actually typed it out on my own, memorized it and it was called Weak People, January 2016. And it was based off the song *Weak People* by Cyhi The Prynce. I thought that was one of the most profound songs I heard of all time because he was just going in on the culture for not really standing up and supporting itself in the right way. And I was a big Cyhi fan at the time, so I was like yo, the people who got on me for correcting the person [that] called me

Black Zaid say he's like, yo, I'm standing up for myself, yo, that's weak. So I was like, I'm gonna write a poem about weak people. And that was my first poem, January 2016.

Brandon Alexander Williams: Wow, 2016. So before then, you were just an admirer of hip hop and spoken word or of hip hop mainly?

Cyde Effect: Hip hop, big Kanye fan. This is around Kendrick, To Pimp a Butterfly era. 2014 Forest Hills Drive was still one of the greatest albums of the modern area at that point. That's the time we were in, so Kendrick was a big influence on my style, Common, for what I say in the book, his Southpaw writing style. And it's the way that he plays around with the syncopation in his writing. So I got introduced and fell in love with hip hop, not necessarily for what they were saying, but how they were saying it.

Brandon Alexander Williams: The delivery.

Cyde Effect: Exactly. So in the opening of the book, that's why I start off *From Patterns to Purpose*. It was the patterns that got me into it, but I had to grow into what the patterns are actually carrying, which I believe and know to be the true essence of what hip hop is or what knowledge is.

Brandon Alexander Williams: It's dope that you said that man. They say that communication is 7% words, 38% non-verbal like tone, and then 55% I think like body language. And so it's like for you to pick up on that and notice that that's a thing, that's something that you zeroed in when you started creating your stuff.

Cyde Effect: It's how they was saying it, Cyhi known for bars, punchlines, x, y, z around the board. And the punchline, that's more so the content of it, but his flow was amazing in wrapping those punchlines together. Common's flow was unorthodox and Kendrick's flow was crazy with the alliteration and syllables. That combination is what I was looking toward mimicking. It ain't no lie, it's just to say that's what I looked up to. Of course, I was a big Kanye fan, but Kanye wasn't known as the best lyricist. He wasn't known as the best when it come to syncopation, it's just overall composition beat x, y, z. That's what Kanye was known for. And I was a big Kanye fan, but as far as me getting into hip hop, it was Kendrick, Cyhi and Common specifically. Kanye, I just listened to him and was like, yo, that song was fire, but nobody out here talks about Kanye being the greatest MC of all time. Nobody's saying that, but I'm talking about MCs here, so that's what got me into it.

Brandon Alexander Williams: Gotcha. Alright, cool. We're gonna jump into this first joint man. Track one is 117 produced by Chicago's own JustCuz , let's get into this joint. **117.**

117

Yo I'm feeling lukewarm
Here's another lyrical dismount
At a discount you could've found on groupon
I'm tired of being known
For trying to only perform and do poems
I'm feeling marginalized
I'm like lightning forced in a bottle
But I'm formed from more than 2 storms
Performing at an open mic
That aint even my true form

See I reek of spirit
Must you spell out his respects
For people to see that he is brilliant
To be the realest, out of my shell for a sample
R E S T in peace I hope Aretha clear it
No filter needed for me to be the purest
King of soul
I say it loud, I'm black and I'm proud of being fearless
Quiet on the set

The most beautiful film is in action
And we just caught in between
Living our lives while our eyes
Stuck on the screen
Not watching as the sun is setting the scene
I'm not mean when I speak,
I just speak what Ameen

The spirit of the real OG's is still deep in my genes
I'm cold pressed even when out in the sun rocking capris
Seeking the highest of seas
Knowing the master chief is me
Cause I am the master of qi
Preaching what a master Achieved

I believe ignoring these natural scene is spiritually fatal
We already present in heaven
So watch me rotate my halo
Then wait for YoDJ to rotate the tables
The way we be spinning around you
You'd think you was seeing tornados
Bass a vibrate peace into the world
And abate a war in NATO
Turn war into a game,
Transform Aries more into Kratos

Heavy metaphors for the matadors
Avoiding the bull
While still looking to pass the torch
Even to a young brother
Not allowed to pass the porch
Summertime holiday
We hope he make it past the fourth

He hopes to survive a local war within NATO
Let's start stopping the wars
With our allies and neighbors
When we call cops they send assassins
Cause we cape the crusaders
We high off the ground
And they need skyscrapers
Cause they be minor
But we know that we major

See we worthy
Be greater
It's in our nature

Whether you know it or not
You love to be close to the One that creates you
Word to the ones worthy to wield the force
Blessed with the lightest of sabers
Not letting the darkness invade em

Once you witness divine signs
And other evident synchronization
Then you embrace it
it just takes faith, patience and waiting
To grow into greatness
Achieve your inheritance
And youll mos def piss off all the satans

Them damn devils
Proud to be heavenly rebels)
If I was at Hajj right now
I would pelt em' with pebbles
Knock em' down another seven levels
And then give em a shovel
Before I tell them to settle

A bunch of witches and grand wizards
Wishing to eat us alive like Hansel and Gretel
They want us tied down or string up
Like they got the hand of Geppetto
Turn us down so much
We can't even turn up to faneto

But I'm the Master Chief
A green leaf achieved that surpassed the keef
A form of woke vocal not mass-produced in a factory
Not seeking to be serenaded with pageantry
I'm pursuing a simple life and not the throne of a majesty

"A brother that don't want attention,
You must be speaking of blasphemy"
"I'm tired of writing of struggle
Just to relate to the crowd

Like that's what poetry has to be"

I'd be lying if I said my life was draped in a shroud
Without even vaping the loud
My head is still able to escape to the clouds
With no need for an assist from the nimbus
My energy be entering other dimensions
We are one
Composed of many
Within a single existence
Woke should be a collaborative effort
For individuals to achieve real independence

No other lines need to be written
I just added this last line for completing the sentence
Now I'm free
From being charged guilty of any convictions
I didn't write this poem for points
I wrote it to make the point
That I'm here to awaken your soul
Without seeking permission
If You Only Knew (21:7)

117 (commentary)

Brandon Alexander Williams: All right, that was 117 produced by Jus Cuz man, yo, it's a lot of fire in that man, we gotta cool off the studio bro. Hold on, I got some lines man, I wanna point out, you said I met you doing spoken word from the spoken word scene, right? Towards the end of the piece you say, "I didn't write this poem for points." All right, you say "I didn't write this poem for points. I wrote it to make the point that I'm here to awaken your soul without seeking permission." We met in the spoken words scene, what does that mean?

Cyde Effect: Hey yo, I don't do it for nobody else, now I do it for the sake of G-d, for the sake of Allah first. And then I do it for me, I do it for my family, and I do it for my community. Community ain't first in this regard, so points, that's a community thing, getting points, props, attention, pats on the back. x, y, z, I don't do it for that first. Like I said I do it to awake your soul without secret permission. You know, these spaces where sensitive conversations need to be held, open mics provide the opportunity to not have to ask for permission to share that information. It's an opportunity for artists and those who want to be heard to be heard. To know that if you write it right, you got undivided attention, right?

Brandon Alexander Williams: Hey now…

Cyde Effect: Just cause you are on stage doesn't mean you got undivided attention.

Brandon Alexander Williams: And if you spit it right.

Cyde Effect: You gotta spit it right. We had this concept in W.O.R.D (Writers Organizing Realistic Dialect), which was the open mic poetry organization at my college, you always heard respect the mic, respect the mic, respect the mic. My boy UYI, U-Y-I, he said what happened to command the stage? We talk about respect the mic, but what happened to command the stage, you know? You can't be getting on the audience just because you ain't catch their attention.

Brandon Alexander Williams: Wow, you got a point.

Cyde Effect: Absolutely. So what I do say is that everything that people do receive from my poetry is a side effect. I got the first effect from the Cause of all causes, y'all get what's left. And what's left, not saying it's to a lesser degree, but I recognize first things first, you know, after the "rest in Peace Uncle Phil" it comes me when I'm writing. (laughs)

Brandon Alexander Williams: No, that's fire. That's dope.

Cyde Effect: Like I said, after G-d, it comes me.

Brandon Alexander Williams: Wow, Cyde Effect, yeah, so y'all get the side effect. That's hard. I like that, bro, and that's dope. Alright, so another thing man, you rhyming like crazy here. So like me, I'm a MC, you're a MC, and the rhyming, the multi syllable rhyming really sticks out to me. Like on this part, on this stanza right here, you rhyme: *"Master chief with surpassed the Kief, factory, Pageantry, Majesty, blasphemy a*nd *has to be."* Tell me what's your thing with rhyming man? Like dude, when you approach it, do you say like, "nah, I can't do hat, cat, ball fall". You know what I'm saying?

Cyde Effect: I don't do, what is it, "roses are red, violets are blue" poems. We don't do that. I've been raised in a culture and environment that respected the MC, respected the art, writing something in a way that nobody else can write it. It's like you might have others that operate in a similar skill form, but it's like using your experience, what you've gone through. The essence of that is what allows you to separate yourselves from everybody else. If you based yourself and what you do purely around what everybody got in common, you know? Yeah, we all write and rhyme the same way, yo, then what's the difference? Why book you when I could book the person that's a thousand dollars cheaper? Cause y'all write the same, y'all write exactly the same. So for me, it's a challenge to myself first. Everybody gets the side effect of that. It's a challenge for myself to do my best in everything that I can do. And *117* was just me getting into that, that wasn't even me. Like that's me coming out the hyperbolic time chamber, it's *117*, that's how I consider it. Every poem that I wrote after it in the next 10 poems in this book, was to build upon that and not stay stagnant, but consistently increase not just in the physical presence of it, but the essence and the meaning of the poetry as well.

Brandon Alexander Williams: Got you. No, that's Ill to hear that man. So we're gonna move on to this next joint man, it's called *Unity*. I'm seeing a Kwanzaa pattern come on, you know what I'm saying? Come here, something like that. So I'm gonna ask you about that after we go into this joint. So this next one is called Unity, also produced by JustCuz shout out to my homeboy JustCuz man. I provided the beats, I did some co-production on this, but he's a talented MC and producer. So this joint is called ***Unity.***

UNITY

Umoja
Our community needs to be rooted
In more unity and free-form composure
So we don't implode from our own promoted overexposure
Shii, we could be like royal roses
Rooted in concrete
With the beauty of a geode cause we've grown from boulders
My flow could shower your mind in reigns-of-gold for hours
Just to quench the thirst of a soul
That floats in an abundant ocean of wokeness

Cause we are one soul
Forced to consume and focus
On the most vulgar of our own surroundings
And you wonder why we love to get high
Our soul fears the very idea of staying grounded
It seeks to reach the heavens
Cause it knows earth isn't the true space
The spirit of mankind was founded
But we still made of it

Every single cell and every Adam came from it
Let me explain something
I could pronounce pronouns like a progressive leftist
But through the most high
I am blessed with encrypted protection
Therefore I'll still use this archaic decrypted expression

Where is our unity?

Eve
Stories of old blame you for humanity's mutiny
But yoU aNd I Both ssslipped into the sssunken place
For sssipping the Tea whY did only you get blamed?
To then only be seen as an object of promiscuity
Ever since then you've only been seeking equal opportunity
Because the form of U.N.I.T.Y you seek Queen
Is bigger than Latifah

It's more likened to the reign of the Queen of Sheba
When she walked across the glass of King Solomon's palace
(27:44)
And saw her true reflection
And then they both submitted
To be seen as equals amongst the anointed people

So where is our unity?
The building blocks of life are made of Adams
Like Eves were too busy building blocks between man and G-d
To be the root of community
Cause where I'm from

A rib is a joke
Like a dude that gets caught cheating but say he was just chillin
And now he wants his baby back
Eve being deceived by the serpent is story men will use to believe
We can do literally anything and still get our lady back

"Hey auntie
I know I killed my girlfriend to get back into the garden
I mean Wakanda
Killed uncle James for betraying my father
Killed your son and I woulda killed your daughter
Just to soil the throne that our family's name has always been a part of
Cause that that don't kill me, make me stronger
So don't push me

*My name is my name cause my hood be filled with Killmongers
Saying hey to Auntie's grieving at funerals that they be the cause of"*

But she will still forgive him
Why?
For the sake of unity
It's not her burden to bear
So she'll pray that Jesus a save him
From black on black crime that is the real form of coonery

And then maybe
Just maybe
One day he'll forgive her
For getting them both kicked out the garden
But that will take some Self Determination
Cause to him a rib is just a joke
That doesn't deserve to be taken seriously
Like UNITY

Unity (commentary)

Brandon Alexander Williams: That was *Unity*. Wow is what I could say. Hold on, there was a line when you said *"Where is our unity, the building blocks of life are made of atoms like Eve. We're two busy building blocks between man and G-d to be the root of community. Because where I'm from, a rib is a joke. Like a dude that gets caught cheating, but say he was just chilling and now wants his baby back."*

Cyde Effect: *<laughs>*

Brandon Alexander Williams: Come on man, what's going on man? Tell us about *Unity*, tell us about this piece.

Cyde Effect: *Unity* was written two poems after I did *117* and that was my first step into writing poetry that I was identifying was truly from me, my experience and what I was growing into. I said that I wanted to use the first day of Kwanzaa as a reference point, which is Umoja or Unity. And I thought about my teachings and our teaching in Islam, that the origins of mankind come from Adam and Eve. Or we don't use the name Eve, but Adam and his mate. And the deception as presented in the New Testament, Old/New Testament about Eve succumbing to the temptation of the serpent and then giving the apple to Adam. That's not in our scriptures, our scripture puts the fault on both of them equally. So in the back of the mind of an individual, that perception can say that it's the women's fault that we are all here,right? That we all got casted out and that type of thing can lead to a downplay of the role of women in society and being what the Jezebels, x, y, z. So I write unity in total to say why are we not united? Because the interpretation of this narration has been taken this way, so I use *Unity* as that. So *"the building blocks of life are made of atoms like Eves. We're too busy building blocks between man and G-d to be the root of community."* The word community in Arabic is "Umma". "Umm", is mother. The literal root word of the word community in Arabic is "mother". So instead of being the root of community, she's building blocks between man and G-d, when in fact, we would say that's the old perception and that's not the accurate perception, so I present it there. And then also that says that if it's the woman's fault that we're in this position in the first place, shoot, I could do whatever I want. It's not as bad as what you did as men.

Brandon Alexander Williams: Ahh like a scapegoat.

Cyde Effect: So that's why I say we could literally do anything and still get what, want our baby back, so I'm talking about baby back ribs, right? Cause I'm talking about the ribs.

Brandon Alexander Williams: Yeah, I caught that, that was hard.

Cyde Effect: *"We can literally do anything and still get our lady back."* So the idea is that we're put in this position of privilege because it's not our fault that we're down here. So we can treat women however we want because shoot, we can't do nothing worse than get kicked outta heaven or be the reason we get kicked outta heaven. So that's the perception that I'm going for and *Unity* is really referencing these themes that can lead to a society that's not united. That's the mindset behind it.

Brandon Alexander Williams: Wow. Nah, that's dope. What I hear from the piece is like, well if this is the case, then this also has to be the case. And the second thing that I'm piecing together doesn't make sense, you know what I'm saying? It's like nah, we should strive for unity. I like that. That's your message. And this right here was really tongue in cheek.

"Hey auntie, I know I killed my girlfriend and get back to the garden. I mean Wakanda. Killed Uncle James for betraying my father, killed your son and I would've killed your daughter just as soil the throne that our family's name has always been a part of. Cuz that, that don't kill me, make me stronger."

Cyde Effect: That whole story that I've taken from Black Panther is literally something that can be interpreted from the exact same story as far as the story of Adam and Eve. Killmonger sacrificing his lady to get back into the garden. Paradise, oh, *"I mean, Wakanda. Killed Uncle James, killed your son"* and it doesn't matter. Look at how much he's done.

Brandon Alexander Williams: Yeah, I remember that. Yeah, dude pulled the gun on him.

Cyde Effect: Look at how many people Killmonger took out and I was known as Killmonger in the city before I started doing my new forms of poetry because I did a Black Panther trilogy. So I was addressing the fact of this infatuation we as a culture had with Killmonger at the time. It's like yo, did y'all not see he killed a black woman. He hemmed another one up while destroying the purple herb. It's like yo, we should not be using him as a point of [admiration]. He's a villain. Oh what, he was the Malcolm X in the movie. No, he wasn't. <laugh>

Brandon Alexander Williams: Nah.

Cyde Effect: So I used the same theme to reference our reverence for Killmonger in the movies and reference him back to the same

thing. We feel like we could do literally anything and still get our lady back. Killmonger does whatever and he should still be the king of Wakanda. No.

Peace

Peace,
We are peace
We are not just a piece of a puzzle
We are the puzzle
Pieced together
By Peace
peace-By-Peace
Squarely rooted back to the planet that keeps us complete..
And our completed planet isn't missing any pieces

That is why I know we are all completed puzzles
That is why I know our peace is important
Because a completed puzzle isn't missing any pieces
So what is it that we think that we are missing

Whatever it is I guarantee it will not bring us peace
But it just may divide
Divide us into pieces of the people
We were before making additional subtractions
Bend us out of shape
To the point that our inner peace begins to look different
Influence our image to the point we can't recognize our form
Because what is foreign cant be forced to fit

Therefore we become forced to fight
Forced to dig
Forced to bury our peace in the dirt

The dirt that once covered that which we now seek
The dirt that due to our fears begins to freeze
Cause we can't find warmth in our degrees
Now resembling dry ice our hearts turn cold

This is the day the eyes-dry and the pain
No longer allows tears to flow
This is the day that'll resemble a drought near the soul
The day we'll recognize that our appetites have taken control
Leaving us full of hunger and forced to wander
Into the darkness with our hands out front
Like a zombie searching for its master
Searching for its mind
That which allows it to seek and explain
It was the pieces from other puzzles
That could only bring us pain
Making us blind to our true royalty
To the point that when we go with the flow
We don't even appreciate our reign

And thats when the tears begin to pour
The tears begin to stain the soils of our foundation
And we began to sink
Deep into a place where we began to think
And we begin to plead

We begin to see that our peace didn't freeze
But it was freed
Buried in the dirt at the beginning of this piece was a seed (71:17)
Squarely routed back to the planet that keeps it complete
It's sprouts into its path of ascent like a tree

A rebirth from the earth that occurred to curb our appetite
It encourages us to BE
And pursue what is right
Recognise what is GREAT
Despite the FULs
In our sight
Cause we don't let their bit of shade

Dim our eternal light
Cause our **Self-Determination**
Ensures that we remain bright
Because we too create life

Because we reflect the son
Because we are like the Moon
Solid as a rock we are the ones that complete this geode
That is our puzzle of a planet
Because we are its pieces
Meaning we are its gems
And this is our gem
Peace

Peace (commentary)

Cyde Effect: It's funny cause out of everything here, *Peace* is the one that was written the fastest, but it's my best one. I wrote *Peace* in two days. It took me four months to write *Faith*. By comparison, I think *Unity* took maybe three, four weeks. It's funny.

Brandon Alexander Williams: That was *Peace*, man, yo, that joint sounds like it's so cinematic man. I don't know where Matrix is at right now cause I don't follow everything, so that sounds like it should be in Matrix six or Matrix five or whatever is next up. So here's what I wanna talk about. I know I usually plug out lyrics and ask you to decipher those. Let me ask you about your delivery on this because towards the end you start getting more and more passionate towards the end. Like yeah, "we reflect the sun." You know what I'm saying? So tell me about that, what made you decide to add what I call tone design? What made you add that tone design to the end of the piece?

Cyde Effect: So Peace starts off somber and *"peace, we are peace."* Just something that one, I'm really planting it in my own mind and the listener's mind; peace. Muslims our greeting is As-Salaam-Alaikum, "peace be upon you, right? Muslim means a person of peace or peace through submission. Aslama means submission. So peace by way of submission, but heavy emphasis on peace. One of G-d's attributes is As-Salam or "The peace." And so for me, I'm starting the poem off peacefully, right? But as I get into it, I start adding disorder. When I start talking about division and burying, that peace is being lost. Now the poem as the energy has this sense of wonder and lostness in it as I'm describing an individual, a family or a community, a whole

society that's trying to find its peace, and it starts bringing in pieces from different puzzles. That's why I love using this puzzle theme for it, and you know, *"can't be forced to fit"*, you know, *"forced to bury our peace in the dirt."* And it's just building up to this point where I'm tired, x, y, z. And it just so happens that this peace that we're burying in the dirt, and I emphasize, and it was a seed, time for that redemption story. Somebody or a teacher of mine was recently sharing how you find this theme in scripture, of course, but you find it in movies as well. You got Batman Begins, you got the Dark Knight, you got the Dark Knight Rises, right? And it's the idea that there's the beginning and then there's darkness, and then there's the coming back from the darkness, right? I just watched the trilogy again, I didn't know they was going that hard in 2005 for Batman Begins (laughs).

Brandon Alexander Williams: *(laughs)* Right, I ain't gon front, I definitely skipped over that. I gotta go back and check it out.

Cyde Effect: So long story short, Peace is a redemption story toward the end of the poem. That's why I use the themes of identifying with nature and the light. Identifying with nature, the light, the strong symbolism. Really emphasizing that this symbolism isn't just a symbol, it's an identification of yourself, of your potential, like how I was mentioning in Success. It's an identification of this isn't just a little thing, this is a growth and a recognition of something bigger coming back into that peace. And that's why I close it: *"And this is our gem."* I usually put my hand on over my heart when I say that, but I'm also emphasizing the gem of life being peace, us being creations of peace by Peace. So we put together peace by peace.

Brandon Alexander Williams: Come on, man yeah!

Cyde Effect: But we're also peace by peace.

Brandon Alexander Williams: Word play.

Cyde Effect: Right? So I go back to that song, but what I like about *Peace* also the way it ends, it can loop on itself. It can start over again because we have to recognize the stories of our lives, just like the cycles of life and death, day and night. Sleepiness and wakefulness is a story of repetition and increasing in that repetition. So *Peace* ends on the same note that it began.

Brandon Alexander Williams: So you get back calm again.

Cyde Effect: Yeah.

Brandon Alexander Williams: Or peaceful.

Cyde Effect: Peaceful

Brandon Alexander Williams: Word. That's dope, man. That's a beautiful thought.

Cyde Effect: That state of energy and excitement and x, y, z can be a peaceful state, or it's supposed to be a peaceful state, keeping it under control, right?

One

ONE
In the name of The ONE
True Master of metaphors and similes
We must choose to
Unite in Peace
As we align into our universal roles and abilities
By not submitting our souls to a universe
That is physical and thus a limited infinity

Through this soliloquy I've expressed
Why it's not logical for me to limit the vastness of ONE
Within the dimensions of our trinity
Cause tauheed taught me to see that ONE
Is beyond the sums of both the seen
And unseen infinite divinity

That provides our sustenance
Through the earth's lusciousness and other amenities
Keeping us Safe and secure like clownfish in anemones
Four times during the solar decline
Our souls climb
As we're kept aware of our
Collective Work and Responsibilities
UJIMA

The fifth begins in the EVEning
But is given as the light of our first day
Threads through the dawn
This enlightens our minds as if the sun

Was a sign that we all could be sons
As we enter
A state of bliss
Nested is this
Pure life and the crisp
Taste of its flavors

Sweetened by The ONE
Baker of bakers
Our clay is molded and shaped by
Thee Who Created creators
The Architect of architects
So now we masons be making
Stories, to guide the blind toward directions
That the faithful are facing

Re assuring seers we're not alone as we practice in patience
Meditation morphing us into neos reborn free in this matrix
Despite the agents whispering fragrance
Into our hearts till we're dripped in temptation
We are jedis forced to fulfill this deen
And root to this real destination
We are saiyans reciting sayings in a similar cadence
That will always span across the sands
For more and more generations
That we be one

Community composed in this system of limitless creation
Our destiny be from the subquantum
To the most galactic destinations
There's evidence in the declaration
Between our system of nations
Systems uniting our atoms, planets, blood
And other consistent foundations

When combining that of learned science
To the wisdom of sages
We follow that logic to conclusion

That we be the one that can sum up and solve this prolific equation
That we Be the one
Created By THE ONE
That Created creation

I challenge you, human
Don't deny your favors (Fabi Ayyi Ala I Rabbikuma Tukazziban) (55:13)
You be The Most intelligent being ever created
That just needs more devotion
To achieve motivation
While outkast
Forced to walk the line between love and hate as you seek liberation
From being whipped into submission
By some of the most cynical of statements
Based in our place that is the pinnacle of creation
Where we're pacing and racing
The ruthless racist ruining our stasis

Making us blind to an inheritance that rewards us for our patience
And so thats why we live to maintain the present in our presence
We learn what truly unites us isn't our skin, face, or our nations
But the source of our essence
If you only knew!
One

One (commentary)

Brandon Alexander Williams: All right. That was One. That's hard. I don't know why it puts me in the mindset of like a video game. Of course none of this is a game. Yo, the rhymes in here definitely stick out to me a lot. Like amenities, anemones, responsibilities. And once again, I'm seeing the theme of Kwanzaa principles in here. Tell me about this piece. Tell me about the creation process of picking and choosing what gos, what doesn't go. How does your writing process go?

Cyde Effect: So One, and I was just saying the word one, I'm not even talking about the poem. It's harder for me to write poems when I'm following themes because I just can't be natural and write whatever comes to me, I gotta be like that don't fit the theme of this piece. Now naturally, if I created a piece that I'm just around it and it starts building, I'm seeing what the theme is. That's gonna happen naturally, but usually it ain't from the jump. When it's from the jump like these, so much more thought goes into making sure everything I say has a purpose. Not just every line, not just every word, not just every syllable, every letter serves a purpose in the poem. There cannot be any misinterpretation of what I'm saying to the best of my ability because I'm very intentional about everything that I'm putting into the pieces.

So that's kind of the big thing for me. And with *ONE*, Ujima collective work and responsibilities. I knew when I saw collective work, our responsibility, I was thinking about just from my understanding and interpretation with scripture was, what is collective work? Community. Our responsibility is to come together as one. So we always talk about oneness and everyone's

connected and the universe is connected as one, its one, its one. This poem is an understanding or a projection of if we talk about all this oneness and G-d says in the Bible how we were made in his image, will we look at physical stature or we will look at the presence or our essential presence as a universe. So will we see that? And by no means does our teaching say that we are G-d, or we are gods. But it says that we are one. G-d is One.

Brandon Alexander Williams: Right, universe, the prefix "uni."

Cyde Effect: Absolutely. So I use this poem using punchlines and metaphors from different sources, but also samples and examples from the universe, the Declaration of Nations for the United Nations, how our blood circulatory systems, everything, operating systems, solar systems. So I say sub quantum our atomic makeup to the galaxies. Why is there such a united consistency there? We are made in his image – oneness. So we are individuals, we have to see ourselves as one, but I'm also using this poem to directly emphasize to understand G-d as One as well.

Brandon Alexander Williams: I love the rhythm. It was like the second to last stanza, I love the rhythm when you said, I challenge you human, don't deny your favors and then you spoke it in Arabic. And like you slowed it down right there bro. What made you decide to do it that way? To read it that way?

Cyde Effect: One. I keep saying one whenever I start a sentence, I don't use a lot of Arabic or quote Qu'ran in its original language much in my poetry cause I don't want to disrespect what we hold in the highest regard. But for this particular line, *"don't you deny your favors"*, the 55th chapter in the Qu'ran repeats that phrase, I forgot how many times, but one verse and then it says that line, another verse it says that line, another verse it keeps saying that. *"Which of the favors of your Lord will you deny?"* And literally, G-d, Allah just keeps telling us everything there is to be grateful

for. And it's like, are you denying this? Why would you deny this? Why would you deny this? Why would you deny this? So I emphasize *"you be the most intelligent being ever created."* Our understanding in our religion is that the human being is the crown of creation. The entire universe was made for human beings to come into existence. Everything in nature, everything from *"the sub-quantum to the most galactic destinations"* is here to serve us and we are in charge of it. We are to come into control of it, but to do that, you have to be fairly intelligent, right?

Brandon Alexander Williams: Yeah. Aware as well.

Cyde Effect: So I'm using that to really emphasize *One* is the affirmation of the individuals that may not see themselves as sufficient in their makeup, but to let you know, one, you're here so that means you're supposed to be here. And if you're here and you're supposed to be here, and you're a human being, you have the potential, as we mentioned in success, to be the most intelligent being ever created. Are you acting upon that potential? How you manifest that potential from every individual's going to be unique to them, but do not measure your capacity as an individual to someone else's. Measure it in light to what the *Creator* says. G-d said you're this, are you gonna deny that? Okay, go ahead and see how it works out, type of thing.

Success

Success
What is our definition of success
Is our success defined by the present conditions
That can change faster and faster every second
Is our success defined by the consistent change
In the subjective truth projected through others
Or Is our success defined by
The ever changing salary that which we happily
Slave our lives over
If so

How will we come to know our true meaning of success
If we're unable to sacrifice for some change in our pride
Our pride is what we thinks keeps us alive
But by locking ourselves in that safe space of success
We're unable to BE

Active
In the process of remaining objective and honest
Unable to be aware of this world's illusion of success
Which seeks to influence the very nature inside us
Through a whisper into our hearts
Refusing to submit to the foundations (2:34)
Of our intuitive knowledge
You see the illusion can be
Ujamaa: Cooperative Work & Economics
While True Success Be Absolute
So True Success Be As-Samad (112:2)

Though a veil thicker than the physical universe
May lie between these words and your conscious
Let me attempt to make our success
More apparent as both a warning sign
And a promise

Success was already present in our presence
Before our birth on the first day
We are to see success like a parent
That grounded us into this earth in the first place
While already in first place
We become further
Rooted into this quantum of success as we fast
This solace of success provides shade during the days of hour last
This is when the complete opposite of success
Is expected for those that reject
Then resurrect their own wrath

Doesn't the success of a diamond lie dormant
Within the darkness of our unpressurized carbons?
Doesn't the success of a coconut palm lie dormant
Within the darkness of our seeded soils?
Doesn't the success of a new Moon lie dormant
Within the darkness of our natural universe?
Through these examples I've shown how logical it is
To know of our potential for success though it will be unseen

Doesn't the benevolence of the vast universe remain present
As we bask in the lunar luminance of our full moon?
Doesn't the brilliance of a coconut palm's journey still have value
As we honor the succulent flavor of our fruits?
Doesn't the ancient process of a diamonds formation
Still have meaning as we marvel
At our modern structure and expression?
Through these examples
I've shown how easy it is to forget about our potential for success
While its manifestation is always present in our faces

This exemplifies how logical it is to know

True success will ensure that it's first acknowledged in darkness
Before manifesting itself as our light
True success is an inheritance
That only through our human nature we'll see as our birth right

Whether or not we know that our true purpose is toward success
Our intentions must remain clear
So how do we make intentions for a destination
We don't even recognize is near
Success be for we that see this poem as a manifest clue
Because **Success**
Be **Creating Faith** in our **Purpose** of **Uniting** in **ONE Peace**
If you only knew
Success

Success (commentary)

Brandon Alexander Williams: That was *Success*. Yo, I like this one. This makes me feel good. It gives me positive tingles, like as I listen to it, you sound so motivated man. Tell me about this joint.

Cyde Effect: So *Success* was falling in line with the fourth day of Kwanzaa, the principal of UJAMA Cooperative work in economics. And I didn't want to be more of an affirming voice of that, I wanted to counter that voice in a productive way that was cautious to identify…I was specifically pointing to economics here and us as a culture, identifying our success based upon our financial status. So that's what I'm directly addressing in the beginning of the poem. And saying that that could actually be counterproductive to what true success is, which in the poem I identify true success to be Absolute or true success is As-Samad. As-Aamad is one of the attributes of Allah (G-d), which means Eternal or Absolute. And in our holy scripture, the fact that it means Absolute, it only appears in the entire book once as an attribute of G-d to really hone in on the point that true success is toward the Creator. And any motion or identification of success in alignment with that will bring literally all other forms of success with it. So for us, and what I'm projecting in this poem is us in our original nature and creation, which I speak about in *Unity*, is already conditioned in the mold of success with its potential. And then that's what I open up to in the poem is the fact that just because you don't see something does not mean the potential is not there. And when you understand that the potential is there for something, whether it's good or bad, when you operate with the best intentions and action, you manifest that best potential.

Meaning it was there the whole time. What changed? I'm the same person.

Brandon Alexander Williams: Yeah, you didn't necessarily pick up new things, you just activated what was already there.

Cyde Effect: You activated what's already there. So I'm identifying what's being activated by default you as an individual or manifest success from the day you were born. And if you do not activate that potential, then you'll never see it.

Brandon Alexander Williams: You say *"success was already present in our presence before our birth. On the first day, we are to see success like a parent that grounded us into this earth in the first place while already in first place."*

Cyde Effect: Right. So we are to *"see success like a parent"*, our first parent, *"grounded into this earth"*, sent to the earth *"in the first place while already in first place. We become further rooted."* So I'm signifying Adam as a seed going into the planet, into the earth, into the material existence to grow, *"rooted into this quantum of success as we fast."* Muslims fast during the month of Ramadan, as we fast we're to hone more into our true essence and into our true purpose of creation. *"This solace of success provides shade during the days of hour last."*

Brandon Alexander Williams: *"Our last"* play on words, but you pronounce it like *"hours"* ?

Cyde Effect: Yes, like the last hour and provides shade during the last hour. This piece that we grow into the success that we manifest, protects us in our last days. Not necessarily just from a scriptural perspective, but even in the days where we're going through some type of trauma. Something that could be the end to one period of our life, something that is a big stepping off point into the next phase of our life. That protection that you gain, that success that manifests over that time can lead to a protection.

Brandon Alexander Williams: Wow. There was a line that stuck out to me. Oh, first of all, I like the whole section where you like, doesn't it? You know what I'm saying? Like don't it? I think that's dope, but no, there was a part where you said:

"...Through these examples, I've shown how easy it is to forget about our potential for success, while this manifestation is always present in our faces."

Cyde Effect: Manifested success already speaking on us as individuals being created in the mold of success, the environments that we're put into in their natural form are already manifest success. Make a better mountain, make a better tree, make a better apple, right? Even if you say, we genetically engineered this apple to be better than all the apples, where'd you get the idea to genetically engineered an apple by looking at an apple. You didn't create anything new, you just changed what was already there, and in essence, you probably made it worse. So what I'm doing in those three examples, I'm identifying the moon, a coconut palm, and a diamond; as being the full moon, a coconut palm that's bearing, and a diamond that we review. I'm identifying those as success manifest. What was once a potential now is in its final form, its most excellent form. We, as human beings, were created with the mold of potential for success. And we are to see our growth in understanding and wisdom as that manifest success. Just like a full moon, a coconut palm bearing fruit, and a diamond. Why? Because we're made of the same things all of those things are made of, same composition. We are to see ourselves in the true elements of the natural world. So would you say a diamond is not perfect? What is perfect? If that diamond is in its natural form, it's perfect. We can cut it up and shape it. All we did was cut up and shape something that was already done. Why? To appease our personal perception of what it is. If we accepted things in a natural form, we'd have more appreciation for ourselves in our natural form.

Intentions

Nia
Our intentions
Form the foundations of our thoughts
Our thoughts
Our sentiments
Form the foundations of our actions
While our actions form the foundations of our environment
But our environments have become the foundations of our purpose
When our purpose should not be subject to change
Because our purpose is who we truly are
Because our purpose is the One Consistent Nature
Found within the spirit of every single being before birth

Containing an innate nature of worth
Like a seed grounded into the womb of this earth
With the potential
To contain the language of a universal verse
Preserved in scripture which is intern rehearsed
And interpreted into a plain language
That I've learned from the learn'd
In order to further nurture the urge
That seeks to emerge from the common person

An urge capable of converting its intuition
Into purposefully manifested divine intervention
Resulting in a guidance

Redeeming the minds of mankind
Into a solidified foundation Based in intention
Which will then form the foundation of our thoughts
Which will then form the foundation of our actions
Which will then most certainly manifest
Our true purpose in the environment
Naturally innovated in the
Foundational Expression of Excellence
That is our human nature
So I beg the question
What is our purpose? (51:56)

If you only knew
Our purpose is a foundation
That we've chosen to build around but not upon
Then becoming surprised when we are used as pawns

In the sinking schemes of the jinvious architect
Mocking our original blueprint
Attempting to tamper with and turn our temperate template
Toward temporary temptations
Turning us back into toddlers forced to tend to our own terrible twos
Because we've been transformed into
This false sense of purpose displayed in our environment

Its empowerment has blinded us
Into a bind
Pridefully assisting in the whisperer's attempt to form an influence
To mentally shift the public
 With a language that is formed into a disguise to uplift
Despite its false foundation that is always fluxing
Until its seduced by the sirens to become the cause its own destruction

Cause where I'm from
Haters are supposed to motivate us
But not to follow them

Yet we do this daily
Our consistent purpose
Manifests first before the birth of a newborn baby
Doesn't their environment like clay shape their reality daily
This consistent nature By Allah was to not be subject
To the side effect of our inconsistent changing
But sadly, this is why many of us
Still resemble a strange fruit that is left hanging
Because we still
Till this very day choose to eat
Of that same fruit that should have been left hanging

Instead of planting our own seeds
Tending to our own roots
Growing our own trees
And farming our own fruits
Because we are our roots
Because we are an extension
An extension of our **Nia**
Our **Purpose & Intention**

Intentions (commentary)

Brandon Alexander Williams: All right. That was *Intentions*. I almost said Nia. Man, so okay, you said a line. You already know what part I'm gonna go to. Hold on, first of all, you said *"jinvious"*. Now listen, I'm not too proud to say what does *"jinvious"* mean. I never heard of *"jinvious"* before.

Cyde Effect: So "the envious one" is a title for satan or shaitan, the envious one. And shaitan in the Quran is identified as a Jinn and Jinn we can identify with that like the genie, that's where Jinn comes from; the Jinn, spirits, like the alcohol gin. So what can stoke an envious spirit, something like that. There's a lot more to go into that, so I just put them together; Jinvious

Brandon Alexander Williams: Nice, okay. That definitely caught on. I was like okay, I don't know that word, I'm gonna look it up or ask him about it later. Then you said:

"Mocking on our original blueprint, attempting to tamper with and turn our temperate template toward temporary temptations, turning us back into toddlers, forced to tent to our own terrible twos." Tell me about that alliteration.

Cyde Effect: So mocking our original blueprint, basically the envious one is envious of our original blueprint, which I spoke upon being success, being the most intelligent being created, I'm gonna use other terms created in excellence. For us a human being striving to the highest form of their excellence is perfection. To recognize when you do your best, if you literally couldn't do better, you did perfect. That's as easy as that. You can't do better

than your best. Can Usain Bolt ever run as fast as he did before? He ran a perfect record for Usain Bolt. Can somebody else do it? Possibly. But for him, your personal best. Everyone's tried by their own personal best. So the original blueprint, *"attempting to tamper with and turn our temperate template toward temporary temptations."* The easiest thing to point to is, yo eat that apple, yo take that laptop that somebody ain't looking at, right? Yo, cheat on that test. So *"tampering with our temperate template"* is getting us to be disobedient or causing us, or inciting us to be against that which is in alignment with our highest nature, morals, and ethics. And *"turning us back into toddlers for us to tender our own terrible twos."* Now like a toddler, we're not able to comprehend what we just did or express ourselves how we want. So now we are just mad because we can't communicate, we can't express ourselves. Why? Because our template has been turned towards something that is not in favor of us.

Brandon Alexander Williams: Would you say that the concept of an intention is like being aware of not just what you were doing or of course, in your case speaking, right? Not just what you're speaking, but how you're being perceived as you're speaking, how people are perceiving you as you're speaking.

Cyde Effect: So that was a direct theme that I use when writing the poem from the jump. It's not what you say, it's how you say it. I took it deeper, why did you say it? The what and the how come after the why. If there's no purpose behind it, what's the point? (*chuckles*) So the whole poem follows the theme on why. So that's what intentions is based upon. It's just the why we are doing things, and that's what I aim for in my poetry. Is not necessarily to get people to do something different or people to say something different. Just be aware and conscious of what you're doing, and then if you choose to do x, y, z, then it's your choice. Cyde Effect's only job on stage is [to ask] if you know what you're doing. All right, you know what you're doing, whether it's harmful or not. As long as you know what you're doing, well I can't force you to do nothing else. We should all just

be aware and very intentional about why we do things or what we're doing, so that's the theme of the poem, is just having that form of awareness.

Brandon Alexander Williams: I would even dare say that like intentions, when we're intentional about things, it gives like a snippet of power, if you will. A snippet of control. I mean if it's done wrong, it can make us drunk, like you're saying…

Cyde Effect: Jinvious. Yes, absolutely.

Creation

Creation
Is a Location
That is capable of displaying the innate-nature
Of excellence legislated throughout alll of its development stages

Creation
Is a Process
Of molding or making the best mould of an object
Capable of holding a breath in its breast To make progress
Toward higher elevations

Creation
Is a Word
Of perfection expressed thats destined to be heard
Through its delicate display of its most relevant verbs that represent
The essence of what's common and shared

In Essence
The COMMON CAUSE
Caused creation
To Be a Word that is Processed in our Location
That which calls for common unity
That which calls for Community
Through both the physical signs of our universe
And our lands displaying this outstanding farm of fluency
This language
Of creation
Is the Spirit of Truth unfazed by the pollution of scrutiny
As the truth of these roots

Can weather your storm with an acute immunity
Witnessed as we watch the trees
Maintain qiyam (stance) on their siraat (path) beautifully

Balanced
By the sabil (their cause) as their branches multiply fruitfully
Just give it up to nature Praising G-d with ingenuity
While we humans can barely gaze toward the path of G-d usually
Thats why we pray five times a day then walk away a Lot
suitably
As the logic lies within conscious beings
Making conscious worship
Truthfully
Thinking what can we do for G-d instead of what can G-d do for me

Cause creation
Face to face says your actions have formed a mutiny
Used to polluted duties you fools are rooted in zoolatry
The globe is getting warm cause you looting the mental mutually
When performing a symphony just to affirm you are true and see
The truth you seek is science
But science will lack its fluency
When not connected to nature
But bias within you and me

The call of nature is creation as learned in the final eulogy
Cause that call is a command to man that demands unity (7:54)
Not born impure
You Were Born In Purity
Before our birth we rehearsed this verse within a surety
Barely a baby yet containing this most merciful maturity
But after birth
Our purpose was hidden
So now we work for our insecurities

As the council of nine seers continue to conjure the trilogy
Slighting their hand over The Word just to justify tyranny
Are you hearing me?

Back in their day
All the saints with their hollow-words weaned
Our creation away from initial victory
Taking creation out of form to treat Adams with their trickery
Remember
"Nukes are not natural yet still the son shines brilliantly
Cause fusion Unifies while the fission dictates a ministry"

Now observe the side effect of this arc of limitless energy
A fusion of ordered synergy moving in symmetry
Morphing a sensitive mortal by peacefully
Keeping his praying soul orderly
The Creator of creations command
Commands this man more and more to act more morally
Forcefully
Like the seasons He phases our nature quarterly

Bear witness to this parable in
The unseen Hand in the land of Oz guiding Dorothy
Walking the yellow road through a garden
Containing more than trees
A whispering witch attempted
Slipping the (red ruby) slippers off her feet

Thats a wicked force from the West
Designed to oppress and attack her modesty
But she audibly gained brains and became a prodigy
Opened her heart so courage could guide her upon her odyssey
Walking upon her path bright with guidance for where she ought to be
Home

There's no place like it
The innate foundational base of our faith thats keeping us orderly
There's no place like it
This creation with its command thats demanding more loyalty
There's no place like it

Allowing those on the cusp of drowning to-stand with more buoyancy
Once concealed in a veil they'll heal and exhale joyously
There's no faith like it

As the second breath allows their breast
To expand more royally
Just as birds in the morning
When the sun is dawning from dormancy
No more sense of complacence
Your faith will enable harmonies
There's no faith like it

Cause there's no faith like home
I guess this is just a reminder because you've already known
That there's no place like home
There is no place like this faith that I'm based in
Because there is no Word Like the Creator's Command
And there's no place
Like His Creation

Creation (commentary)

Brandon Alexander Williams: All right, that was *Creation*. Yo, so hold on, we gonna jump to these lines. I highlighted some lines. First of all, you're killing these rhymes, man. I'm such a fan of well rhyming. So that's always the first thing that catches my ear.

Cyde Effect: I always say well-written. "That is well written"

Brandon Alexander Williams: Yeah, that is well-written. It's a rhythm. It's the rhythm of it that's undeniable, you know? So the first line that stuck out to me, I like how you broke down this word, like in front of someone's face. How it says *"in essence, the common Cause caused creation is a word that is processed in our location."* This part right here. *"That which calls for common unity, that which calls for community."* Like common unity and community. It's like, oh, that's what it means. You know what I'm saying? Another thing that you said, first of all, you were killing these: suitably, truthfully, mutiny, zoolatry, mutually, you know what I'm saying? Fluency. You were going crazy, and one rhyme in you said *"thinking what we can do for G-d instead of what G-d can do for me."* Selflessness. Like…

Cyde Effect: Literally, when I say the language of creation, what is it? *"This language of creation…"* I don't remember the line right now, but the emphasis for that line is the fact that creation projects a word. It projects education and knowledge. Name one thing you can't study? And then with that studying, look at how you can improve things and bring them into a higher form. So just like how I spoke of *Success*, us coming into this [life] with this potential, and then we grow into this manifest success, nature in and of itself, it's a body. The universe is a body of potential. And only the most intelligent creation that is meant to come as a body to potentially grow into its most excellent form, can take nature from its potential into its most excellent form by studying nature. *(laughs)*

Brandon Alexander Williams: That's fire.

Cyde Effect: So a skyscraper can't build itself. People pose the question, look, this beautiful iPhone after billions and trillions of years, could this ever make itself? Will the sand come together and form glass? No. Will the chips, no. No. The mind of the human being was able to create that because that is what the human being is made to do for themselves and for their environments [in order for] their communities to grow. So creation gives us the instruction on how to do that, not to build iPhones, but to build ourselves. And who put this education and word into creation, the Creator. That's what creation is for. So the emphasis is on verses that speak on *"with Allah belongs the creation and the command."* There was creation and then as the creation is studied, you extract the command in what we're supposed to do. So what are we supposed to do? What do we do for G-d? Read His creation. Act upon it. Instead of what? Yo G-d ain't doing this, this and this. Everything's there.

Brandon Alexander Williams: *"Thinking, what can we do for G-d instead of what can G-d do for me?"* Nah, that's fire. There was a line that stuck out, you said:

"Before our birth, we rehearsed his verse with an assurity barely a baby, yet containing this most merciful maturity. Yet after birth, our purpose was hidden. So now we work for our insecurities."

Cyde Effect: (*grunts*) Unh!

Brandon Alexander Williams: What?! *"Our purpose was hidden, now we work for our insecurities."* That's hard. Because I get the imagery of like, you know, our insecurities working for it. It's literally like slave driving. It's like nah, you gotta do this because this ain't enough.

Cyde Effect: Yes.

Brandon Alexander Williams: And what does that line mean to you?

Cyde Effect: First of all, this is all scripture. I've been studying the Qu'ran for the past couple years. Through my experience that I've grown in and reading and studying and having my teacher, that's what came out to make it something that the average person can hear. So our purpose was what? Barely a baby.. So I'm speaking about, you know, us coming down as a seed of potential. When I say we rehearse this verse, there's verses in the Qu'ran that say that before we were even born, we testified that you are our Lord, you are our creator before we even came to this planet. But when we came here, all right, your literal purpose in life is to come into that understanding on your own, but it's instilled in your nature. So your body's gonna call for it, but our purpose was hidden. And another meaning for Jinn means the one that hides; hidden. So our purpose, who hid it? The one that's envious, I'm gonna hide your purpose in these temptations. *"Our purpose is hidden, so now we work for our insecurities."* We working for everything against us and not for us by the ultimate hater.

Brandon Alexander Williams: Wow. That's super hard bro. Yo, hold on, I'm counting these rhyme endings. You said "Ministry, energy, symmetry." Then you switch to "orderly, morally, quarterly." And you said, "Dorothy." I like that cause that's how

Dorothy is spelled. Most people just say "Dor-thy." They don't say "Dorothy." Quick side story, right? So one time in fifth grade, I actually failed a spelling bee because they said, how do you spell sophomore. And for those of you that don't know, it's spelled soph-o-more. It's an extra "o" in the middle, but no one says "soph-o-more," everyone says "soph-more." And so they're like, oh, spell sophomore. I'm like, "that's easy S-o-p-h-m-o-r-e." They're like, "ehnt!". I'm like, what you mean? And I look at the dictionary, I was like, you dirty rotten… But no, that to me is like the weeds of like creativity when it comes to rap and spoken word. Like you knowing to say "Dor-o-thy" right here as an option, that boasts a certain level of lyrical IQ, that's like, I know what I'm doing. Like not just I know what I'm doing, but I know what I'm doing better than a lot of y'all. You know what I'm saying?

Cyde Effect: So background on that, going back to when I first got into it, remember Kendrick, Cyhi and Common, for me, wordplay, the lines, the structure was everything. I wanna write so fire that nobody would dare come to me and say, you should have put a beat on that. Now, I don't mind having a beat on it, but nobody is gonna say it needed one, right? "Man, this just needs a beat."

Brandon Alexander Williams: You hear the rhythm.

Cyde Effect: Put the lines together, use the word and make the words their own beat, right?

Brandon Alexander Williams: Yes.

Cyde Effect: And you know, the beauty is in the structure and x, y, z and that's the thing, that's Tuesday…(laughs) So it's like for me, it is like yo, all right, now make it mean something and make it mean something else.

Brandon Alexander Williams: Yeah cause when you get past OD'ing off the rhythm of how I'm doing it, now go ahead and crack that open and see what's in there.

Cyde Effect: There you go. There you go. And that's the thing, it's like, you know, something that's really sweet but it's oh wow, this is really healthy. I never would've thunk it.

Brandon Alexander Williams: Yeah. Nah, that's fire. We're gonna move to this next joint man. This next joint is called **Faith**. But man, you sticking these syllables bro. I can't wait to hear how this one sounds. Alright, here we go.

Faith

Faith
Is the foundational base
That allows both security and trust
For you to truly believe you be safe
In your space even amongst these days

With their altered darkness
Faith
Enables the unlocking of optics
Through sparks
From The Cause that are the start of the process
Like shocks
To your heart bringing you out of the darkness
In order to brighten your day

Just in case
You come into contact with a fight
That in a way makes you say
I think I just might want to pray
But these fights are the problems
-
These fights are moments of an unnatural darkness
A darkness
Making it seem as though you have run out of options
These fighting forces are first formed by then affirm the imposters
Like commandments but they conjure a darkness
That is conned up and then conjured by the unconscious

That forced us

Into submission by first forging
Thee - most - materialistic facade for The Father
That we accepted
As they then projected their false light
Onto the skin of a man that was olive
Real faith
Is what phases waves
Of the sons light to walk on top of the waters

Reflecting
A pure human essence
That is just following orders
That are often observed in us orphans
Privileged to witness how the creation of nature is flawless
These are the side effects of reading
Or rewatching my performance recordings
You cordially
Start acting according
To the most excellent expressions of a soul in the garden
Before you even enter a coffin

Faith
Is what causes our hearts to soften (13:28)
Faith is what causes us to consciously pause for caution
Our nature
Is to elevate through the stars
All by guidance from The Cause that inspires our conscious
To no longer crawl beneath smog or sleepwalk through the darkness
Darkness
Brought by the false light of flames
Blazing and broad
Chock-full of toxins

Cause like moths to the flame
Some souls are the same
Seeming insane when seeing this same chock-full smog as the

Psalms of David or Songs of Solomon
Or any other problem solving pollen thats
Relayed by way of The Cause
Through lots of oxygen

But smog
Behaves according to the deserts doctrine
Smog is what makes the waves of a deserts mirage more opulent
Causing our relapse back into this mirage of intoxicants
fostering
False facts of the first facade
That are always befogging our competence
And don't we always watch as this

Breath of death
Inflate then escape the chest of scriptural novices
That make made in His image translate into ye are gods and goddesses
What side effects of this cause are being caused as a consequence?
Well
We begin only seeing the source of true knowledge as
Whatever we say it is
Our acknowledgement of G-d adjust
Just as the temperature of whichever day it is
Horoscopes
Crystals
Sage
Palo Santo and Astrologist
Have become our deities
Plaguing us like intoxicants
That make us more and more incompetent
As they put our day at ease

So isn't it awkward?
How we've allowed the systems in power to misdirect our posture
With scripture that is obviously doctored
That was formed by first altering the talks of the Prophets

Using the scheme of what is popular
To start plotting a mantra
Keeping us in the dark
As they prop us up-on a soapbox at an auction
Like orphans
Abused when adopted
By this artificial form of faith from a light that is toxic

Their light
Is not just observed by the eyes in our sockets
I swear from apples to apples
We just keep on biting the bondage
Just as smog is clogging our sinus
False light causes our blindness
False light disguises the righteous
False light surmises social media likes with the pious
Vertical spikes in the stock market start to make us admired
Just as social capital collapses our hearts till the day that we dying
Dumbfounded and destined for the door of the dearly departed

Covering our shame with what's discarded from gardens
All while inhaling this smog of the bothered
Smog of the ones that choose to live this life as a hostage
The ones that are Praying to go astray and potentially die a gnostic

If you only knew
You needed these diagnostics
Unity Peace One Success Intentions Creation and Imani
Faith

Faith (commentary)

Brandon Alexander Williams: That was faith. Yeah, you snapping on all of these, but see, you snapping on this one too. A part that stuck out to me, you're doing a lot of homophones and homonyms and I like that. I like that because once again, that boasts IQ, so like *"seeming insane while seeing the same"*, once again, like know to do that and know how to employ it in your writing. There was a part where you said:

"Horoscopes, crystals, Sage, and Palo Santo, and astrologists have become our deities. Plaguing us like intoxicants that make us more and more incompetent as they put our day at ease."

Cyde Effect: *(laughs)* I mean, hey…

Brandon Alexander Williams: Because most people pronounce it deity (dee-ih-tee). People pronounce it that way. So it's like you knowing "if I pronounce it *this* way, I can say another thing."

Cyde Effect: And that's the thing. There is a pronunciation. Somebody says, "day--tee." People say "day--tee". So I'm like deity… Day at ease… *(laughs)* It tells itself there. And that's the thing, like I said, no word is wasted. I don't waste words. And when I put that together, it was a very significant thing for me to be able to do. Cause all of the poems in the series, the seven that I wrote, were a gradual buildup to me to be able to be confident and more comfortable being clear and not necessarily that my intentions are in trying to get y'all to convert, no it's just see what you doing or assess yourself to be acknowledging of what you're doing. Shoot, my faith in G-d puts my day at ease too. But I'm also not saying my G-d is another deity. I'm not acknowledge my G-d as a type of intoxicant or our G-d is a type of intoxicant. But, you know, it's for that of an individual. People know of Rumi being a well profound poet and scholar particularly in Islam. My thing is like, taking Islamic poetry and only thinking of it in the eyes of those from the east and Middle East is like, yo, this is a Black American male that was born and raised in the community that grew out of the Nation of Islam. What does our poetry sound like? What does my poetry sound like in that light? So, you know, that's what we are getting through, through all these pieces.

217

"I'm tired of writing of struggle
To relate to a crowd like that's what poetry has to be"
3 years ago I got co-signed by Rhapsody (2019)
She called me a real MC
That affirmed that the Master Chief was always within my capacity
Now as my halo rotates
I hold my hopes high in the heavens while escaping the gravity
Of a warning
Sent to save our sacred souls from catastrophe
Bringing this modernist age of religious apathy
Back to the roots of community that founded humanity
As my cup runneth over
You witness the stream of my flow
Connecting yours back to the straight path
Using nature supported social logic rationally

I could teach your rabbi how a covenant Ends
As a golden calf is replaced by golden caps in your cavities
I could teach your pastor bout the present past
And how Adam and Eve were always seen as equal
And not unsatisfactory
I could teach your yogi how heaven is a physical experience
And in this life were tested with the smallest taste
Of it's immaculate alchemy
For example:

During my euphoric metamorphosis

I heard a word of choice from a voice
More notorious than Morpheus
Some call it voodoo and some may call it vodoun
Regardless
Thats the moment I entered the cave
Emptied my thoughts then sought the cocoon
Where I was fed the good word but never off of a spoon
As the shock Sparked in the dark
The sonics started to boom
"This is not a game
You need to start taking this seriously"

After those words I was no longer a coon
This regular show character (regular show)
Was blessed and chosen to know the G-d of the toons

All of my contradictory logic was then dead and buried
Like false gods in a tomb
When that myth of the human mold is exposed and unfolded
The Word ensures your soul becomes woven immune

Alcohol, acid, smokeless fire and shrooms
Are no longer needed nor consoled or consumed
After the shock of lightning brightened my senses heightened
Likened to the boldest lotus that floats solely in a golden lagoon
I perfumed as I bloomed
From that womb I emerged connected and intune
With the inherited heirloom
From our prophetic platoons truly
Crossing them burning sands and cruising the dunes

Now I'm a part of the faculty
Our spiritual nature phases as we're walking the moon
Bringing this baptized baby
And the bathwater back from the balcony
The religion of Muhammad Ali
Is bringing this Malcolm up out of me
Despite the NOI's foundation being based in a fallacy
It was made as a counterweight to the god complex

That to this day still enslaves our slavish mentality
But from it's womb
It rebirthed the purest form of Faith based in reality
Are these lines not proof of an immaculate alchemy?

Just read the Qur'an with an open heart
To achieve a universal view, of your personal gallery
Find an unlimited salary
Finally put some real spirit within your spirituality
Our souls seek to rise
So for our hearts and minds
I'm just here to remind you, how to achieve your mastery

And to remind you
Affirms that you were knowing before
You see Hamz was just passing the ball on the court
Now the Cyde Effect is here to settle the score
If you only knew
Your Halo too
Is what you've forgotten to be grateful for

Warner Brother

I'm a Warner Brother
Sent here to warn a brother and to warn a sister
That **My Life Is A Bar**

The master of metaphors and similes
Exposes who we truly are
Just like the amount of money we spend on a car
A latte at Starbucks
Or a chain the same color as the winged dragon of ra
Knowing damn well that these things
Are things that we can't afford

Like how you bout to resort through this full course (meal/class)
Like at Red Lobster
Knowing you barely can be affording my claw
Cause I got that cheddar bae
Meaning a portion
Of my authored corpus is worth more than a portion of stars
The light from my writing a start dropping your jaws
Like you swimming with sharks

Or zombies walking from the white right back into the dark
As the throne of iron transforms this man into a Stark (iron throne/man)
Before winter fell back when I started building my ark (story/reactor)
"Is he talking HBO or the boat"

Don't matter just know that my lines are shocking
Cause they're written in sparks (intuition)
An AED from the heart
I'm giving jumps with written lines
That are jumbled and jarred
So you don't get drunk in the mind
Like Barney Gumble stumble and fall
So before I deliver Moe
Of these Ales
I'm a just let y'all sit at that bar

I'm giving gifts when I separate my statements
Thats how I present a clause
Cause when I plant this written material
Up out of this we - grow - spiritual
Shout out to T raking in green cause when she - go lyrical
Y'all attach to that heat that seep from the frost

Cause we be cold steel
Putting the crowd on game as that fire be going off
But soo chill

I thank G-d everyday I'm protected
By the Source of my soul's Will
Keeping me vaxxed
Cause the side where I'm from (east side)
Be keeping me soo I'LL (southern Illinois)
Who want the smoke
These bars come out my souls grill
Like Lola Ladae in the kitchen I'm cooking a soul meal
I want my wife to see life like Phylicia Rashad
But with no Bills

If she know herself first then she'll know that these goals real
From knowing the Seal she'll know that he know the Seal (33:40)
As signs are delivered
She be wondering
  "How he not blind from the light when seeing the vision"
Of mountains upon pegs firm in their fixtures (78:7)

Cause she know-this heals (notice hills)
She know that I'm gifted.
She'll already be dipped in whatever I'm dipped in (2:138)
Whether thats the Well of zam zam
Some liquid light, or a sip of some lipton

My spirits remain patient cause my life is consistent
After I learned I can't do this over
My life has been different
Then I learned I could do this sober
My writings been different
Even when up close
That web of lies are keeping y'all vibes social distance

I'm Miles Morales
With that exaggerated swagger
Y'all know y'all want whatever this spider lifting
Despite the tension
A hero's mission is to strive through the struggle
Not fight the villains
Despite the damsels in distress
Oppressed by the hieroglyphics
We've been gifted
To lift them myths into higher dimensions
Unfold them into sunflowers (Sunflower By Post Malone)
So we're not feeling dandy as we lie in division
With our hands on a manual (Quran)
On how to handle the writing of critics

We out in the wild wild west with our will's Smith
And lessons to deciphen blood from the cryptics
Definition
"Thats a teaching thesis decrypted"
We vicegerents
Taking advice to deal with the vice in our visors
That are vibing different
We the ones planning this world on a matt
Groening while we write The Simpsons

Knowing there's no such thing in life thats just Like a coincidence
We hoping the heathens seek and then fight for redemption
As they're souls seek to breathe
We hear them wheezing as their light is dwindling
From their original stasis
Back when their light was as bright
As that hair that was as white as Gwendolyn's (gwen stacy)

We must learn to control our passions as the fires kindling
Cause what was in the beginning will be in the end again
It's written pen to pen
On the liquid lens within us descendant dividends
Crafting our minds so we can live again like enderman
So now you wonder
Who is the next one that the ONE is sending in again??

See
This that testament testing if you know your worth
This that forbidden fruit again and I'm avoiding the curse
Like what's up danger? (What's up danger By Black Caviar and Blackway)
I'm Adam's baby boy in this war
Covered in Earth
By taking a leap of faith
I became enabled by knowing my worth (Cain and Abel)
Yet to carry my cane cause Cain a kang captivated with conquering
For the satan accursed
"But what does that mean?"
Even if my poems ended in a happily ever after

They'd still find a reason to
Despite a man and to despite a verse (Spider man enter the Spider Verse)

Now I'm Peter Parker
A professional resurrected
Code-named "The Gardener" (2:35)

Ring wrapped in a web of my all elite jargon
To fight these "sinister sicks" masked in Mysterious marketing
I see the Sandman scoffing at Vulture's hawking
At Electro charging yall folks the most bogus of bargains
While Kraven on stage raging at Doc-oc stating its awkward when
He performing on stage and see Cyde Effect walking in

Halfway through his performance the whole crowd start talking and
Saying:

"Last time Cyde Effect came up short"
"Nah, he did that to prove that he could stand up tall again
You see, some calling him some kind of
Manifest spiritual ordinance for the audience"
"His words contain the world, but be as wide as a web"
"And while we stuck in that net" (www.net)
"I think he stuck himself to the wall again?"

But guess what
Just when you think I'm cornered
You can never guess who I'm calling in
Shout out to my sensei
The one in the cardigan (Brandon Alexander WIlliams)
Dressed so fresh and so clean you think that he going golfing
And my other sensei
Got the power to put the titans out they tower
Cuz the spirit that she got is way more taller than (T Spirit)

Where we stand We able to remain more tolerant
Our bars descend from a higher plane.
That's music made by a taller band
Real students of the game with my name
Would never reuse the name taliban
I'm here to separate the real from the fake
And force the fake in the toilet as we flush it
To never be seen nor saw again

Islam is my game

And my Muslim name says if you say the same
While making a stain then guess what
Warning

I'm calling in
Dishonor on you
Dishonor on your cow
Mu-shu with more lines
Like a bad dad with more rhymes
I'm disowning you all again (mulan)
It's time for y'all to start talking to G-d again
Cause y'all a living testament of how the sons of Adam
Can be raised up and still fall again

I'm using my jinn to ignite fire to force a spider sense
To tingle on top of y'alls call-a-jinn (Collagen)
Y'all a sell ya souls in a second
But won't put a couple bucks in the bucket for offering
Yeahh I said it
You millennials
Y'all embarrass me
Like who else wants to be a millionaire
Yall too prideful to call a friend
Or survey a real life audience
But a play 50-50 for the meaning of life
While desperately thinking that y'all solving it

If you really cared to know what's next
Then you'd just check the prefix (the pretext/scripture)
To know the suffix (the effects)
Of reading the autobiography of X
But not caring to know of the Lord that he loved best

So you must love stress
Feeling depressed
The answers to all your questions
Have been sealed in your chest but reveal to the blessed (2:7)
The next plane (paradise)
But with no jets

Thats what's really keeping me feeling refreshed
You feeling lost please know this map is written correct
Cause when I speak I reveal an address (reveal and address)

Both men and women confusing real freedom
With skin being revealed in a dress
-
I'm not vain and don't say I'm insane
I'm just saying I'm not ashamed to say that I'm not the same
Cause like the words of a false poet
A false sense of freedom can come off just as potent
Seeming important yet impotent
Like how we associate 44th potus with progress
While we as a culture continue eroding

Low key this the flow that got me noticed
I'm Killmonger decoded (manga decoded)
With no subs (no substitutes/subtitles)
We talk in dub (in wins, original language)
As we win in this game of language and we aint even wrote it
"You said Cyde Effect got a writer ghosting?" (ghost writer)

Maybe
The flow of that Arabic a get you feeling aerobic
Like you floating In a boat that a chauffeur drove in an ocean
Close to the soul
As you hope to know of the One who composed it
Haters be feeling insulted like
"Cyde Effect being bogus cause he low key exposes"
A truth they already knowing
But be scared to promote cause they live a life in emotions
Taking a toll on they growth although they try to do yoga

They still stretch, pose, and lie (posers, liars)
Just to dive in them potions
Dazzled in dope when ignoring they know his writings the dosage
Needed for light in their life to increase their shock with the voltage (devotion)
Just by invoking the soul's closest consultant

He awoke the devoted
While walking the valley
With just a staff, a poem, and a cup overflowing

Now together we growing
And going to higher places
I got a hard drive upgrade now I live in a solid stasis (ssd)
Where I diagnose with a wisdom for the rest that are tired waiting
It'll take time
But unlike a bad doctor I'm aint losing no patience
This is how the young one that once created cynical statements
Is now commanding the stages
Enabling greatness with the most blatant of fragrance
By telling truth to the patrons ignoring the call of the satans

The ones too busy to praise G-d
Cause they too busy praising they greatness
What do I mean when I state this?
I'm a creator with enough sense
To acknowledge that I did not create this
It's divine decree already described in the pages
I just opened the book and wrote
What my eyes saw it was stating (lived experience)
Please
Find your truth in my statements
Don't attempt to limit the metaphors that I'm making
Cause the same applies to the stars in the night sky as you're gazing
When reduced to just zodiac signs and horoscopes for entertainment

I transform performance stages into enlightenment spaces
The fourth wall is a stage this warner brother is breaking
Unlike psychedelics siking your psyche into a type of complaisance
This is an open invitation
To: *Those seeking a gate that goes beyond manifestation*
And I know these words relate to you
Cause they're from a scriptural basis

I just have to play my cards right as I go fish on these stages

Cause knowledge is knowing I'm a king
But wisdom is knowing a king is still lower than Aces
So let's just call a spade a spade
As we protect our hearts
From the diamonds and clubs
That seek to suit us in enslavement
Before we back to the start
So I've warned my brother
And I've warned my sister
To See Our life As a BAR

Warner Brother (commentary)

Brandon Alexander Williams: Who do you think you are, man? Who do you think you are to come into this studio, write this 10 minute piece full of fire. What's *Warner brother* man? Tell us about it. What does it mean?

Cyde Effect: My middle name is Nadir, which means a Warner. In scripture, particularly Qur'an, warners are identified as the Prophets or Warners. Not calling myself a Prophet here, but I am recognized, actually, no. I am acknowledging the fact that it's in my name. My first name Zaid means increasing or abundance. My middle name Nadir means Warner, and my last name Hameed means a praiser of G-d. So increasing in my warning of praising G-d. I take that literally into my writing, so *Warner Brother* is like, I'm a Warner brother. So the theme of it follows Warner Brother Studios. I wanna reference a whole bunch of movies, a whole bunch of references, and all of them are written about basically worship, praise, and being aware of how you're moving on a day-to-day to your Creator. Last point that I make on that is just the fact that *Warner Brother* was a challenge for me to say I could write a 10 minute piece and keep a crowd's attention. I want to refine what I did in *Warner Brother* and be able to write a 20 minute piece, an hour long piece. It's like there's no limit, unless we limit ourselves to it. You know, that spark hasn't come, but *Warner Brother* was written and memorized in 17 days.

Brandon Alexander Williams: Wow. I remember you spitting it in the parking lot of, what is it now? City Foundry?

Cyde Effect: Yeah.

Brandon Alexander Williams: I remember that. You was like, "yo, I got this joint." He was like, "it's kind of long , but check me out." He was like, "I shouted you out at it," but no, this is dope. It's even doper to read. That's what I just enjoyed doing right now while I was playing it, reading through it. And seeing how certain lines was like, oh, he meant it this way. You know what I'm saying? And I think that's the beauty of having print media, print words in front of you in addition to hearing it. You said a Simpsons line and you said Matt Groening, who's one of the creators of Simpson. I remember seeing that on the credits.

Cyde Effect: Right, the point I wanted to make also, back to Kanye, when he said, on Jesus Walk, you saying *"if I talk about god, my record won't get played."* I said I'm gonna write a 10 minute piece about G-d using what I know from my experience and what you saying there, like, what we all know about "the Simpson predicted this, the Simpson predicted this." It's like, did they predict this or is it just some random coincidence? And I start the poem off, after that line, I said *"there's no such thing in life that's like a coincidence."* Maybe they didn't do it intentionally to predict the future, but what's the odds of that? There ain't no odds. The fact that it happened is evidence of something else. What's the odds that we happen to live in the "Goldilocks Zone" of this solar system on this planet that has this ozone layer and is in this perfect point in the universe, da, da da da da. The odds are so immaculate. It's like that thing they pose with if you put a whole bunch of monkeys in a room with a typewriter, will they make Shakespeare? No. It's like, is it possible? What is it they say? If you take a bag full of like Scrabble letters, it's just full of infinite letters. You throw them on the floor, it's not going to fall down and be a George R. Martin book. Is the possibility of them falling that order there, but is it possible that that will happen? Absolutely not. And the fact that the circumstance that we are in as human beings in this entire universe, is it possible that you just throw the universe in a hole and it happens? Yeah, but that's not possible. At the same time, the fact that it happened is evidence of something else.

Brandon Alexander Williams: Someone's involved or something's involved.

Cyde Effect: Absolutely. The fact that it happened is evidence that there is control there. It's like there's this great balance because I would say the universe is balanced on the tip of a needle. What can allow that to be?

Brandon Alexander Williams: You say,

"This is how the young one that once created cynical statements is now commanding the stages, enabling greatness with the most blatant of fragrance by telling the truth to the patrons. Ignoring the call of the satans. The ones too busy to praise G-d cause they too busy praising their greatness. What do I mean when I state this? I'm a creator with enough sense to acknowledge that I did not create this". I like that.

Cyde Effect: *"Is divine decree already described on the pages. I just opened the book and wrote what my eyes saw it was stating."* Absolutely. And I'm not speaking about the book as just scripture here, looking toward explaining the universe earlier, communicating the body of knowledge. Books communicate bodies of knowledge. If the universe creation of command is putting words, things we can study x, y, and z, the universe itself is a book. I just opened a book and wrote my eyes saw it was stating through my experience x, y, and z. I'm just writing this down. The source material, the Cause, right? I had nothing to do with that. I'm just the effect of that and then y'all getting the side effects.

Brandon Alexander Williams: Side effects, that sounds like a great point to end on, man. Thank you for your time, bro. This is beautiful. Man, I can't wait till the book is finished. *If You Only Knew.*

Cyde Effect: *If You Only Knew.*

Brandon Alexander Williams: I like that. Of course, my brain goes to Aaliyah, like (sings Aaliyah), but of course you don't mean it that way, but it's like, if you only knew, it's kind of like… I could tell you so much more and I do in the book and in these poems.

Cyde Effect: Absolutely. I guess kind of to wrap it up with just the title *If You Only Knew,* you have many verses in the Qur'an that explain or detail something just immaculate and profound and it just ends like *"if they only knew." "If you only knew." "If you but knew." "If you only understood."* And it's one of those things that is like, no matter how many times I say something to you, you're not gonna get the whole thing. And it's like if you only knew, type of thing. So I use this book as a story to my younger self and the experiences I had to go through to get to where I am and explaining the life that I have now. I start the book and I say, you know, *"if you could give advice to your younger self what would you say?"* I'll just say bro, if you only knew. Like I can't detail none of this to you, if you only knew. And so that's the idea for the book, is writing to myself, but also those that I'm writing to. It's way more that I can't even comprehend that I don't even know. And it's like, I'm just giving you a small snippet of this and y'all aren't even gonna catch all of this. It is like, fill in the gap with if you only knew. And that's how we wrap it up.

Brandon Alexander Williams: That's fire man. So where could the people find you, man? Tell the people where they can find you at?

Cyde Effect: So you can find me on Instagram @ Cyde Effect, that's @cyde.effect. When you go to that Instagram page, you can find a lot of these recordings. You can find a link to purchase my book as well. Release 2/17, February 17th, 2023, that's the plan. Located down in Atlanta, Georgia, looking forward to getting my

feet back wet in these performance spaces. And the idea of it is just to express the excellence that our community was brought into for the sake of not just ourselves, but for all of us as humanity. So you can find me on Instagram, and all my links will be there.

" 7/8/2022 "

Made in the USA
Monee, IL
09 February 2023

27314988R00073